Wealthy by Choice

Wealthy by Choice

Choosing Your Way to a Wealthier Future

Ilene Davis, CFP®, MBA

Tablet Publications

TABLET PUBLICATIONS • COCOA BEACH, FLORIDA

Wealthy by Choice
Choosing Your Way to a Wealthier Future

Published in the USA by:
Tablet Publications
2023 N. Atlantic Ave., Unit #226
Cocoa Beach, Florida 32931
Phone 310-610-3634
email orders@tabletpublications.com
www.tabletpublications.com

Tablet Publications is an imprint of Seaworthy Publications, Inc.

Library of Congress Cataloging-in-Publication Data

Names: Davis, Ilene, 1950- author.
Title: Wealthy by choice : choosing your way to a wealthier future / by Ilene Davis, CFP, MBA.
Description: Cocoa Beach, Florida : Tablet Publications, [2017]
Identifiers: LCCN 2017011625 (print) | LCCN 2017021427 (ebook) | ISBN 9781892399939 (e-book) | ISBN 1892399938 (e-book) | ISBN 9781892399908
(pbk. : alk. paper) | ISBN 1892399903 (pbk. : alk. paper)
Subjects: LCSH: Money--Psychological aspects. | Wealth. | Finance, Personal.
Classification: LCC HG222.3 (ebook) | LCC HG222.3 .D39 2017 (print) | DDC 332.024/01--dc23
LC record available at https://lccn.loc.gov/2017011625

Table of Contents

Quick Question

Here's my question: If you had to choose one of the following for your future, which would it be?

1. **BE** Rich
2. **LOOK** Rich

Years ago, I was talking to a mortgage broker and she commented about how many couples she had worked with who couldn't qualify for a $200,000 mortgage even though their income was over $100,000 because virtually all their income was already committed to various kinds of payments.

In "The Millionaire Mind," "Secrets of the Millionaire Mind," and "The Top 10 Distinctions between Millionaires and the Middle Class," the authors postulate a key reason some people become rich and others of equal income and talent do not is that when confronted by similar obstacles, challenges or opportunities, those who become rich respond differently than those who don't. For example:

- You're eligible to invest in your company's 401K plan and get "free money from the company match, but don't want your money "tied up."

- You're in your 20's, retirement seems "far away," and besides "you might not live that long," so you wait until 50 to start investing for retirement.

- You want to be accepted by people who earn much more than you do, so you buy a new car every several years, live in a house that costs 50% of your income, and pick up the dinner check for everyone so you will keep being included.

There are dozens of similar choices others have made so at age 55 or 65 they found themselves with no option (financially) other than to keep working as long as they are able.

When it comes to building wealth, the best plans in the world won't lead to greater financial prosperity any more than no plan at all if you don't actually IMPLEMENT the plan. And not only implement it, but BELIEVE that you have the ability to reach your desired goal, and that even small investments have the potential to be a source of great future wealth.

While the choices offered in the question at the start are not mutually exclusive – that is to LOOK rich and BE rich - unless you have very high income it can be difficult to do both.

As you read the stories in this book, and hopefully implement some of them into your daily life, in the end, only you can decide which CHOICES to make as you go through each day.

Whether you accumulate the wealth needed to consider yourself to truly "BE rich," or just enough for it to APPEAR you are rich may ultimately depend on your answer to the question at the start of this chapter.

> ***"The easiest way to remain poor is to pretend to be rich."***
> -attributed to Henny Youngman

The Letter That Truly Made My Day

– and was the "kick in the butt" to get this book (*that I started back in 1999*) finished!!

A couple months ago, I responded to a request from a reporter looking for people to interview who had accumulated more than a million dollars. I responded, and ended up being one of five people across the country that were profiled in the article. I also earned less than the other four who were profiled in that article.

What I did not know, until we received a call from my boyfriend's son out in California, is that the article had been one of the stories that appeared on the front page of Yahoo.

In response to the article I received an email from a lady who had read the article, was struggling financially, in debt, and as best as I can remember, seemed really discouraged. We talked briefly by phone, and I encouraged her to read a book, "The Richest Man in Babylon," that I recommend to anyone who says they are struggling financially.

I tell them to pay particular attention to the story about the couple who was going to sneak out of town in the middle of the night because they were deep in debt, but instead were advised to implement what I call my 70-20-10 plan. (This concept is included in the chapter of this book titled "Highway 70/20/10 to Wealth.")

Well, suddenly I received the most incredible letter. It brought tears of joy. Here is the letter:

"Dear Ilene:

I first contacted you as a result of reading about your efforts to save in Yahoo's "How I Saved $1 Million" article.

You told me about a book, "The Richest Man in Babylon" which I initially borrowed from the library and then purchased at a wonderful bookstore in Hayward, CA. I know it's taken a long time to write and say "thank you" but I had to find the right card!

You gave me something more precious than money.

Throughout my life, I have <u>always</u> resented the fact I <u>have</u> to work. Through reading the book you recommended I discovered a sense of purpose which boosted my self-esteem. Nowadays I walk around with confidence and very rarely does the little voice in my head speak up to point out my weaknesses / failures / lack of beauty, etc.

Having suffered severe depression, and even attempting suicide last year, you cannot imagine how much you have helped me.

Thank you for taking the time to reply and recommend the book. I even stopped procrastinating; stranger still, people often say "hi" or talk to me when I walk at break or lunch times!!!

Wishing you the best.

I have been recommending "The Richest Man in Babylon" for as long as I can remember. I've found as I talk with clients that have saved a lot that many had read the book prior to meeting me. And those who have read it upon my recommendation have similar comments to those referenced in the letter above.

While the language of "old Babylon" can be a little confusing at times, the stories are easy to read, and each chapter is a story in itself.

I strongly encourage anyone with a desire to be financially independent to INVEST their money in buying, and their time in reading, this book. I also encourage reading it with a highlighter, and then reviewing what you highlighted. I'm confident you will find both the time and money spent a good investment.

FEW PEOPLE PLAN TO FAIL, BUT SADLY MANY SUFFER THE CONSEQUENCES OF FAILING TO PLAN.

Dedication

To my father, who taught me most of what I know about saving for the future, and gave me the common sense to actually listen at a time when few children listened to their parents. (*Amazing how much wiser he seems the older I get.*)

To the friends whose conversation I happened to join who were talking about getting a job as a stockbroker, and when I said that sounds interesting, looked at me and said, "you should be the one applying for that kind of job."

And to my mother: who got me started investing when most children have only spending on their mind, and who opened the door to me becoming a financial professional by introducing me to the manager of her own stockbroker and recommending he consider hiring me as a stockbroker.

To my many clients whose questions and concerns gave me the foundation for the examples you will see throughout this book.

And to the authors of the books I've read through the years that have been a source of inspiration and education for me as both a financial professional and personal investor.

Disclaimer

IMPORTANT INFORMATION TO READ BEFORE YOU CONTINUE

Dear Readers:

WEALTH IS NEVER, EVER GUARANTEED. *You can do all the saving you choose to do. You can make what you feel are wise investments. You can do your best to manage your money wisely and live within your means. But all you need to do is look what happened to many wealthy Cubans or Russians or citizens of other nations to see that just because you accumulated wealth, doesn't mean you will always have it. For some, it may be that spending every dime they make and dying owing others money is the lifestyle they choose. But for those who have enough faith that they will have a future, but also believe social security and pensions will not support the lifestyle they hope to enjoy without having to work, this book may offer ideas that can make working for a living truly an OPTION.*

For over 30 years as first a stockbroker and then a Certified Financial Planner® (often shown as CFP®) I have believed that even with social security and a pension, most clients would not have sufficient income to maintain their desired lifestyle for the rest of their life once they stopped working.

Based on that belief, my goal has been to help clients accumulate the personal assets (investments) they will likely need to "fill the gap" between what they expect to receive in social security and other retirement benefits, and the income they will need to afford their desired lifestyle should they be unable, or just not want, to work.

That is, to have enough in investments able to produce sufficient income on a regular, ongoing basis, or that could be sold and invested in investments that can reasonably be expected to produce income on a regular, ongoing basis to provide the income you would need to do what you want, when you want, with whom you want for the remainder of your life, without having to "work," with "work" defined as: *something you do because you need the income it generates to afford the lifestyle you want to enjoy. "Work" is something you would not do if you had all the money you felt you could ever spend in your lifetime.*

That does not mean you don't volunteer to do things others might consider work. It doesn't mean you don't do something you enjoy doing and get paid for it. For example, one friend is a consultant. He loves to help people be successful. He loves to golf. So, he is designing a business that he will do coaching for business people on the golf course. He will be doing what he loves to do, but making money doing it, helping others, and just golfing with different people each time instead of the same group of friends. It doesn't mean he won't golf with friends another time, but this would be what I refer to as "not working" even though income is being generated.

Other friends who have retired are also working, but again, they do it for "fun money," and if the job disappeared the next day, it would not affect their financial ability to do what they enjoy doing.

The stories and examples throughout this book are actual ideas I have shared with clients, and many of them have implemented, through the past 30 plus years. Many of them are from my own life. Others are stories clients told me.

As this book is required to go through compliance with my Broker Dealer, one of the subjects that came up during the compliance evaluation is the use of the terms "WEALTH" or "FINANCIAL INDEPENDENCE" as being "PROMISSORY." That some people may believe if I use terms such as those to be the "result" of a proposed saving idea, some readers might assume "wealth / financial independence" is GUARANTEED."

Let me make this clear: **FUTURE WEALTH IS NEVER, EVER GUARANTEED** (see chapter "Easy Come, Easy Go")

The purpose of this book is simple:

To help readers see how, if they CHOOSE to IMPLEMENT any or all the ideas in the book, and INVEST all or part of what is SAVED, and these invested savings EARN SOMETHING over the period they are invested, there is the POTENTIAL / POSSIBILITY to accumulate income producing assets (which for simplicity I call WEALTH).

IMPORTANT DISCLAIMERS:

- Material discussed does not reflect investment fees or expenses and if deducted, performance would be reduced.

- The HYPOTHETICAL examples used in this book are for illustrative purposes only and do not represent the performance of any specific investment.

- Case studies are hypothetical examples of the various approaches that can be taken to assist readers with their insurance and/or financial planning needs.

- The results depicted in this book are unique to the hypothetical cases presented, and should not be construed as a guarantee of future results or situations.

That said, I hope you will find at least some of the ideas throughout this book are something you can apply in your own life, or that you feel worthy of being shared with others.

Wishing you a happy, healthy, fulfilling, and prosperous future.

Ilene Davis, CFP®, MBA

Cocoa FL

Ilene Davis is a Registered Representative of Royal Alliance Associates, Inc.

Securities and advisor services are available and offered through Royal Alliance Associates, Inc., Member FINRA, SIPC. Financial Independence Services / Ilene Davis, CFP® does not offer legal or tax advice. Please consult the appropriate professional regarding your individual circumstances. Certified Financial Planner Board of Standards Inc. owns the certification marks CFP®, Certified Financial Planner (T) and CFP® in the U.S., which it awards to individuals who successfully complete CFP Board's initial and ongoing certification requirements

> ***"Wealth is the ability to fully experience life."***
>
> —Henry David Thoreau

Nothing is Guaranteed

(C) 1993. Ilene Davis

The **CHOICE** is YOURS

NOTE: There is no guarantee if you invest through the years that you have more, or even as much as you invested, but it is more likely you will have more assets to help finance your post-work years than if you don't invest at all.

Financial Intelligence

It's been said that what you don't know, can hurt you.

In a world where having personal financial resources (i.e.: MONEY) can often mean the difference between having an option to live life as YOU choose, or having to live under the daily control of others, it can be essential to understand the basic underlying concepts of what you need to do to become financially self-supporting without "work" income, and how those basic concepts intersect with your daily life.

Americans today are taught many ways to MAKE money, but few have been taught how to make that money work for them. Yet this is the real secret to wealth, for at some time in life, the stream of income from working will most likely end, and without money working for you by that time, you will likely need to depend on family, friends, charity or government assistance to survive.

The lack of REAL understanding of some basic principles I feel are essential to accumulating the finances resources to live life as you wish, whether or not you CHOOSE to work for pay, is what has lead me to write this book.

I was at a meeting the other night with a group of people supporting an organization whose mission is to help women become successful entrepreneurs, and when asked what I hoped to offer this group, I said it was my passion for "financial literacy."

Because one of their goals was to not just help their clients become financially "literate," but to become "fluent," they had decided to change the terminology to "financial fluency."

Feeling bad about correcting me in front of the group, the president of the organization came over to apologize, and while I told her there was no need, it got me thinking.

This is the result: our goal should not be just financial literacy, or financial fluency, but financial INTELLIGENCE - that the clients of this organization (and hopefully the readers of this book) gain the kind of knowledge (think of the CIA gaining "intelligence" about enemies of America) that will enable them to understand not just how to save money or invest, but to truly understand what it will take for them to protect their future from dependence on government, charity, or their children to maintain not just a bare existence if they are not working, but a truly enjoyable and comfortable "work-optional" life.

I think the first place to start is to understand how "intelligence" about a couple simple but critical concepts can affect a person's future financial wellbeing. I call them the "3 BASIC QUESTIONS."

I actually came to seek these questions, and their significance, in 2010 when I read an article in the December 6, 2010 issue of "Brevard Business News," a local weekly business paper.

The headline of the story by Patricia Sabatini of Scripps Howard Service was "Couples' math skills add up to more wealth, Rand Corp. study finds."

Personally, I think a far better title would have been "1.5 MILLION REASONS YOU SHOULD BE INTERESTED IN UNDERSTANDING THE MATH OF FINANCE." Regardless, it got MY attention.

The article referenced a study by researchers at the Rand Corp. which found when spouses correctly answered 3 math questions, family wealth averaged $1.7 million, versus $200,000 when neither spouse answered any of the 3 questions correctly.

That was a difference of $1.5 MILLION. Since that was a rather large difference, it sparked my curiosity.

That article did not provide the three actual questions, or where they could be found, but with such a huge difference in wealth, I started searching via Google to find them, and once I figured out what to search for, found they are available in a variety of places on the internet.

And the hunt was definitely worth it when I realized that things I had taken for granted for years as common knowledge (like "The Rule of

72"), were actually not that well understood by many others, even many with advanced college degrees.

The group in the study - participants in the Health and Retirement Study –were a nationally representative sample of Americans over 50 years of age. For the 2004 study, a special module developed by two professors, Annamaria Lusardi and Olivia S. Mitchell, was created dealing with retirement planning, testing the understanding of what the professors called financial "numeracy."

The results were reported in a paper they co-authored in 2006 titled "Financial Literacy and Planning: Implications for Retirement Wellbeing." (Lusardi, Annamaria and Olivia S. Mitchell (2015). "Financial Literacy and Economic Outcomes: Evidence and Policy Implications. Journal of Retirement Economics. 3(1): 107-114. Available at http://www.pensionresearchcouncil.org/publications/pdf/JEL_FinLit_LusardiMitchell2-12-14.pdf)

Meanwhile, I want to share with you the 3 questions that were included in their module and added to the study (answers provided below):

1. Suppose you had $100 in a savings account and the interest rate was 2% per year. After 5 years, how much would you have in the account if you left the money to grow: more than $102, exactly $102, less than $102?

2. Imagine that the interest rate on your savings account was 1% per year and inflation was 2% per year. After 1 year, would you be able to buy more than, exactly the same as, or less than what you could buy today with the money in this account?

3. Do you think that the following statement is true or false? "Buying a single company stock usually provides a safer return than a stock mutual fund."

The first question tests your understanding of the concept of compound interest. The second question tests your understanding of the concept of inflation, and the third tests your understanding of some investing basics.

I've shared these questions with dozens of friends, fellow business owners, clients and even politicians. Some look at me and say "you're kidding" because they find the questions so easy, but others just look at me with a lost look on their face. For some of the latter group, if they really think about it, they can figure it out, but others finally admit they have no idea, or just guess and hope they are right.

The reason I bring this up is that the minute I start talking about numbers, or show someone one of my charts, many will say "I just don't understand math," or "that's too hard to understand."

You only need to review the results of that survey – that those who could answer the three questions correctly had an average net worth of $1.5 MILLION MORE than those who could not to see why understanding those basic math concepts could be worth the time to learn.

This book can only offer you the tools to build wealth. It cannot force you to learn to understand how to use them or force you to IMPLEMENT what you learn.

Again, the CHOICE, is yours.

Don't let lack of knowledge
be an obstacle on your path to wealth.

Answers to the 3 questions:

1. More than $102
2. Less than what you could buy today
3. False

My Own Story

While I was blessed with wonderful parents and a wonderful childhood, I've lived a pretty average life.

Financially, I've mostly been on my own since I was 19 when dad and I disagreed on where I would go to college when they moved to another state my junior year and I went were I chose, but at my own expense.

When I got divorced in 1987, my investments were worth about $70,000. Between then and 1999 when I started writing this book I made a LOT of financial mistakes. My 50 shares of Microsoft I sold in 1986 for around $5,000 would be around 14,000 shares today worth over $800,000. I loaned (and lost) $30,000 to a "friend" who turned out to be a fraud. I was in bad relationships that harmed my income.

Still, by 1999 when I started putting together ideas for a book, my investment portfolio (*thanks to a really good stock market*) was worth almost $1,000,000, and in spite of terrorist's attacks in 2001, the financial scandals of 2002-2003, and the financial crisis of 2008, as of June 18, 2015, my investment portfolio exceeded $3 million.

I owe much of that to my parents. While they didn't give me money, that taught us to save, and invest. I recall a joy-filled childhood. Most of our vacations were spent in tents instead of hotel rooms. We went to parks and beaches instead of Disneyland. I'm sure we went out to dinner but the only memory I have of that is of a place called Horn and Hardart where we could choose our food from these little glass windows.

The main thing I remember is being loved, but also disciplined, and I believe a large part of who I am as a financial advisor, as well as what I've accumulated in personal wealth, is due to something my dad said to me when I was a 19 year old.

At the time, he was an executive at one of the largest companies in town. His peers were buying THEIR children cars, so one day driving to work with him during summer break, I had asked him when he was going to buy **me** a car. More than 40 years later, his response is fresh in my mind:

"Just because I earn the money doesn't mean YOU get to spend it."

While I admit at the time I didn't appreciate that particular lesson, and called him names, said he didn't love me, that he was selfish, and so on. Through the years, particularly since becoming a financial professional advising others, I share that story with friends and clients because I'm confident that had he given in to my whining, I would not be in the financial position I am today.

And that was only one of dad's lessons (see chapter titled "Teach Your Children Well"). Even though I worked during the summer to help pay for college, as long as dad was subsidizing my college costs, I had to account for every penny I spent. But thanks to dad, I learned early in life that when it came to money, choices often had to be made between what I wanted "now," and what I might want in the future.

In my early 30's I quit a "job" to work on commission as a stock broker, with my mom for many years asking when I was going to get a "real job."

Until the past five years or so, my income was relatively moderate, but what I did do through all the years is save, and invest, and suffer through a lot of bad investment decisions.

I believe a key advantage I had in accumulating wealth was an understanding of the power of compounding, a love of investing and understanding that accumulating wealth – for most people – can be accomplished by investing modest amounts of their income, year after year, throughout a typical working career.

I started on the path to being a middle age millionaire when I made a crucial observation: while I was trading this stock for that – usually selling just before what I sold went up and what I bought went down and making very little forward (financial) progress, my clients were investing on a systematic basis, leaving their investments alone, and most importantly, were making money.

I share "my story" because I feel it is VITALLY IMPORTANT for you to understand one simple fact - I am really no different than you. I did not start a high-flying internet company, I did not inherit the money, I didn't win the lottery or any other "lucky windfall." I had problems just like you. I made investment mistakes just like most people.

And what I believe, from personal experience, is that if you truly want to be a millionaire, barring some major health issues and expenses, the only obstacle is likely to be you, and what you do with your time, and the money you earn throughout your life. The past is a great teacher, but don't let it be your master. The reality is we remember the past through our own "filter." Change that filter and the past could look totally different.

The key question is:
"Are you willing to make the sometimes difficult choices needed to create the wealth needed to be truly independent?"

Note to Readers

A KEY ASSUMPTION OF THIS BOOK is that you desire to reach a point in life when young enough to enjoy it to have enough PERSONAL financial resources to maintain your desired lifestyle whether or not you work for pay.

This book has been almost three decades in the making, and as pension plans are closed and retirees increasingly become responsible for providing for their retirement years, I thought it might be a good time to share ideas developed through those thirty years.

Through the years, I've found in spite of a variety of books, magazines and TV shows about finance, it appears little progress has been made in Americans being more financially able to support themselves if they lost their job.

As I turned 65, and knew I had enough money to retire comfortably, I decided this was going to be my year to write a book to share what I have learned (and applied) over the past 30 plus years that enabled me, as well as many of my clients, to be able to live an enjoyable, fulfilling, work-optional life, in hopes it could help others do the same.

I realized that in many personal finance books I had read through the years, I hadn't found one that provided the "math" to do critical personal finance calculations. In other words, they didn't provide easy to use tools to help their readers calculate "how much they would need" to be able to afford their desired retirement or other financial goals.

This book is a compilation of various ideas, thoughts and tools I used to help myself and clients through the years and have not found in other personal finance books or magazines. Because some of the information from years ago is still relevant, you will find some information is based on articles I read in the 1980s or 1990s. They are included (with current information when I could) because I think they provide valuable perspective. For example, while the "stock market" (using the S&P 500 index) increased from 138 in January 1983 to 1258 by December 2010, an almost 1,000% increase during which there were 7 significant drops in that market according to a chart from Reuters.com, the median net worth of U.S. households in 1983 (adjusted for inflation) was $88,000. But in 2010 had dropped, to $77,300.

I believe failure to accumulate wealth at a time anyone with wages could have invested in an IRA – often getting a tax deduction as well – had less to do with lack of income, and more to do with lack of knowledge. This book seeks to provide both knowledge, tools, and ideas for those who want to not just have more money, but know how much is needed financially to live a truly enjoyable, fulfilling, work only-by-choice life for the remainder of their lives (*while they are still young enough to really enjoy those years*).

FOUR CATEGORIES OF RETIREMENT AGE PEOPLE

1. Those obligated to keep working to support themselves (and their loved ones)
2. Those who can't "afford" to quit working, but who are forced to quit due to illness, disability, etc.
3. Those who keep working past the retirement age they would like to retire for other FINANCIAL reasons
4. Those who can afford the lifestyle they desire whether or not they work

Creating Your Path From Wages to Riches

© 2010, By Ilene Davis CFP®, MBA

Every day the CHOICE is mine
Whether to win or whether to whine.
Whether to spend or whether to save
Whether to be fearful or whether to be brave.

The CHOICEs are mine, it's up to me
Whether I'll be poor, or financially free.
Whether to be rich, or whether to be poor
It's up to me what the future has in store.

Every day, I know I'm free
To CHOOSE the future awaiting me.
So, bottom line, in the end
My financial future on me depends.

An understanding of different investments
Is something I need know
To design the composition of
My wealth portfolio.

Compound interest
Can be friend or foe
Depending on if it's of debt
Or investments designed to grow

There are some basic rules
To becoming financially set.
Saving part of all I earn
And staying out of debt.

Investing those savings
So they work for me
In emergency reserves
And diversified categories.

Whether I can afford the life
I'd one day like to have
Will most likely depend on me
And my willingness to save.

The daily CHOICEs I make
On how I spend, save and invest
Are keys to my future income
My financial freedom nest.

It's important to have
Both dreams and wishes
But it's daily discipline
That's can turn wages into riches.

It's never too soon
to start making wealth enhancing
CHOICES.

Thoughts on Life and Money

Following are some thoughts on life and money you might find of interest:

- The goal in life should be to enjoy it.
- Invest money to spend time the way YOU want to spend it.
- Everyone has a boss – hire your money to work for you.
- Investing = converting current income into future income.
- Wealth = choice.
- Wealthy = able to do what you want, when you want, without having to worry about how to pay for it.
- Money = the ticket to life's necessities, and niceties.
- The key to financial success is not doing "without," but understanding the "trade-offs" of actions taken or choices made today versus the consequences or results in the future.
- The goal is not retirement but living future DREAMS.
- Instead of "save," or "invest," use "find jobs for" your money.
- If you do not yet have enough invested to support your desired lifestyle your most IMPORTANT JOB is saving as much as you can and giving each dollar a "job" working for you.
- From a 76 year old: "old age is when life collects for the mistakes, accidents and misjudgments of the past."

While there is no guarantee that thinking rich will make it a reality, reading about those who started with little but created significant wealth will give you some "wealthy" ideas to pursue yourself that could start you on a similar path.

The CHOICE is yours.

> ***"Too many people spend money they haven't earned to buy things they don't want to impress people they don't like."*** - Will Rogers

My Personal Philosophy

I believe life is too short to make all the mistakes you could make yourself – it's usually easier, less painful, and often less expensive, to learn from the mistakes of others, and life is too short to have to get up each day and do something you don't enjoy doing just to put food on the table and a roof over your head.

I BELIEVE if you don't have enough money working FOR YOU, you may be stuck doing something you don't enjoy to be able to afford even life's basic necessities.

I BELIEVE by investing a portion of each dollar you earn, you are planting "money trees" that can produce new income FOR you instead of needing to be produced BY you.

I BELIEVE if you are dependent on others for your daily needs, you ultimately will need to keep THEM happy, losing the freedom to be your "true self."

I BELIEVE if you don't need the income or principal from your investments for at least seven years (and preferably not for ten years), stocks are an appropriate investment.

I BELIEVE that when it comes to investing, being able to understand, and control, your emotions is critically important.

I know sometimes, what you want to buy right now is more important than what the money you will be spending, invested, could buy in the future. Some of your choices will enhance your wealth – others won't. That's life. I've made many foolish and expensive CHOICES in my own life. I'm also human. This book is full of personal biases. Knowing my personal biases can help you filter out some of those biases.

When it comes to investments, I believe being either too aggressive, or too conservative, can both be obstacles to your financial success.

I've developed what I call the "waterfall portfolio." It is comprised of a series of "ponds," with money flowing between them as directed. The concept works for just about any age or income level and is based on the belief that the time investments would have to "work" before they are needed for either income or withdrawal is a key factor in how much to invest in different financial categories (i.e.: cash, bonds, stocks).

It works as follows:

Emergency fund: there should be enough money in cash equivalents (*investments that can be liquidated at any time without risk to principal*) to pay at least three to six months of basic living expenses. In addition, if you are planning a major purchase within the next two–three years, unless you plan to borrow the money (*and pay interest*), the amount needed for that purchase should be in cash equivalents as well.

The remaining investments would be in a series of "ponds." The amount in each pond is based on how much money you need to fill the "***gap***" between your income and expenses at different times in the years ahead.

The ultimate goal of this concept is that barring a major and unexpected expense (for example: a major medical expense), you should never have to sell an investment at a loss.

Think of being in a restaurant where when the water in your water glass drops to a certain level, the waiter refills it. The idea of the "waterfall" portfolio is that as various investments in your portfolio earn income, or distribute capital gains, those distributions are deposited into the "pond" that covers your "gap" needs for the next one–three years.

The philosophy behind this approach is that certain investments "historically" (*and remember, past performance is no guarantee of future results*), have less risk of loss depending on the time frame involved before that investment might need to be sold.

Each "pond" would have investments based on the years until you would be likely to need some of the principal.

- The first pond would generally be invested in a savings, checking, money market account or CD. It would have enough money to cover the difference ("gap") between your income and expenses for the next one-three years. (*If you are working and your income exceeds your spending, then other than your emergency fund, you may need very little in this "pond" other than what is needed to pay your monthly bills.*)

- The second pond would hold assets you don't anticipate needing as a source of income for at least two years up to seven years. This "pond" would be invested in investments that are likely to have low volatility during the period, and income generated would be added to the first pond to maintain a two-three-year cash "cushion."

- The third pond would be for assets you don't anticipate needing for at least five years and potentially as long from now as 12 years. Again, distributions could be distributed to lower ponds as needed, or reinvested.

- Finally, in the fourth and last pond, would be investments focused on longer term growth that may have significant price volatility in the short term, but historically do not lose money in periods of 10 years or more.

Financial Independence Defined

Money should never be the most important thing in anyone's life – your health and well-being are infinitely more important. But the fact is that money is a necessity in the world most of you reading this book live in, and in the real world, money problems often create people problems that can ruin health and destroy relationships.

As we get older, financial problems become more acute if we have not prepared ourselves financially for a world where working for income might not be an option.

The vast majority of retirees today cannot live COMFORTABLY on pension and social security alone. And the cost of living tomorrow will probably cost more than today. You do not have to be an economist to know that most of your basic living needs cost more today than they did five years ago, and you can be fairly certain most of those costs will be higher in another five years.

Financial independence is a concept, not a number. It's the concept of being financially able to CHOOSE whether to work or not - without sacrificing your desired standard of living. It's about being able to afford to enjoy leisure hours doing things you WANT to do, not things you NEED (for the income) to do. It's the ability to afford to choose where you will live, and with whom. The ability to choose who you will associate with, or not.

I'm sure each of us has our own definition of what "Financial Independence" means, but based on 30 years of working with clients of different ages, income levels, backgrounds, etc., what it all seems to come down to is this:

The ability to afford to do what you want,
when you want,

with whom you want,
without having to do something to pay for this life when you would rather be doing something else.

In other words, as Richard Bach's Jonathan Livingston Seagull says, it is "the freedom to be YOURSELF, here, and now."

The goal of this book is to provide you with information and ideas to make that life possible, regardless of your income, providing you have the time to realistically do what is needed, and the WILL to do what it will take (*as long as your actions do not harm or abuse the trust of another*) to achieve that goal.

While there are always exceptions, for most people, doing something that violates their conscience to achieve a financial goal in most cases means they have gained material success, but lost the most important possession they have – THEMSELVES!

If you can't get up each morning and like the person you see in the mirror, is all the "stuff" in the world really worth it all?

There are few instant solutions to accumulating the financial resources to "live life on YOUR terms." A high income does not ensure it. If you spend all, or most, of what you earn, you are unlikely to have the financial resources you need to replace your income should that need arise.

Financial planning is like planning a trip or solving a puzzle. We each have different goals and desires, we each have different paths we can choose to reach our goal. What we all have in common is that achieving many of our goals ultimately requires MONEY.

While neither you nor I can change what has happened to you in the past, you CAN use your past experiences, good and bad, to learn from and build on to CREATE the future you seek. If you CHOOSE to do so.

If you don't know where you are going (financially) how can you ever know how to get there?

If you don't know how to get there, how can you plan to arrive on time?

When You Come to a Fork in the Road…

As the title of this book suggests, the CHOICES we make in life can often be a step on the path to greater wealth – or not.

I have been a fan of Yogi Berra's "yogi-isms" for decades. Two yogi-isms I've shared with clients for as long as I can remember because they always seemed to apply so well to retirement planning are:

"Be careful, because if you don't know where you are going, you might not get there."

and

"Be careful, because if you don't know where you are going you might wind up somewhere else."

What I learned last year is that one of my clients, who with his family have become like family to me over the past several decades, is actually the nephew of that same Yogi Berra, his mom is Yogi's sister-in-law, and his kids are Yogi's grandnephews and grandniece.

When this nephew and his wife joined us for part of our vacation last year, and we got on the topic of Yogi's quotes, he asked if I knew the story behind Yogi's "when you come to a fork in the road ... take it." Needless to say, I didn't, so he told me the story:

They were going to Yogi's house, located in a neighborhood off a main road. The short road into the neighborhood dead-ended at a cross street. When they asked Yogi which way to go, his response was "when you come to a fork in the road, take it."

You see, the road they were facing was actually a circle, and Yogi's house was on that circular road about equal distance from the fork, so it didn't really matter whether they went to the left or the right, either way would take them to his house.

It might be nice if no matter what choices you made in life they would take you where you wanted to go, but the reality is, life is not that simple, and your money doesn't work that way (*at least not most of the time*).

Once you make a CHOICE on how to use your money, you may not be able to get where you wanted to go if the "road" you took takes you someplace else and you don't realize it until it is too late to get back "on track."

The reality is that many of the CHOICES we make throughout our daily lives, even minor ones, or ones that seem to have no financial significance, could dramatically affect our ability to accumulate the financial resources needed to finance the lifestyle we seek to enjoy.

MONEY IS YOUR "TRANSPORTATION" THROUGH LIFE.

While there are always exceptions, for the majority of readers, money is needed to pay for what each of us need, want and desire in life.

There are four sources of money:

1. You working
2. Your money (or someone else) working for you
3. Charity (which ultimately is money someone else earned that is given to you)
4. Theft (illegal and not a nice thing to do)

What is Your Passion?

Are you now doing what you truly want to do in life each day, or are you having to work doing something that is not your true PASSION, your DREAM LIFE, in order to pay the bills, have some fun, and hopefully put money aside for a future that provides more free time to pursue your true passion?

The reason I ask this early on is that ultimately, the only logical reason that you would be reading a book like this is if you aren't quite where you need to be financially to have that dream life you would like to enjoy.

Moreover, if you don't know WHY you are doing something, it can often be hard to stick to a plan. When it comes to not buying something you could enjoy today, the more you can "SEE" that future life you want to have, and KNOW how much that life will cost, the easier it will generally be to make the CHOICES that might be needed to make achieving that goal a reality.

Ultimately, each time you make a CHOICE in life, it will come down to a simple question you will need to ask yourself: *"Will this action help me reach my desired goal, and if not, is doing this action more important now than my long-term goal?"*

In the book "Start With Why," by Simon Sinek, the author proposes that if you know WHY you want to achieve something, your mind will focus on HOW to achieve it, and then on WHAT need to be done to make that goal a reality.

While some people are lucky enough to win the lottery, or invent a great product that millions want to buy, the majority of us will need to have a real plan to achieve our financial goals. And a foundation of that plan should be the WHY of what you want to achieve. The "why" is the PURPOSE, the REASON that you want to achieve your goal.

When it comes to creating a Master Action Plan (M.A.P.) to afford the "freedom to be yourself," to have your dream life, to live your passion, a key foundation in being able to calculate the resources you will need is to know very clearly, "what" that lifestyle will "look like." That will help you focus on WHY it is important, TO YOU, and "what" that lifestyle will cost, so you will be able to determine if you are making progress toward your desired goal.

Moreover, the author suggests that a key reason most businesses fail – and the same can be true of individuals - is that passion alone won't make things happen. It is the "driver," but it needs the structure of a plan, a M.A.P. That's where the "hows" and the "whats" come into the process.

And one thing that can increase your odds of achieving your goal is to spend time with people who care about you enough to help you stay on course, rather than distracting you from it. If they know the WHY, why that is important to you, and are true friends who believe what you seek is good for you, they will be willing to help you achieve it.

Knowing WHY you want to accumulate wealth may be one of the most important tools in actually making that goal a reality.

Arkad's Lesson

There are dozens of great books on wealth and personal finance, but the best in my personal opinion is "The Richest Man in Babylon," by George S. Clason.

The stories (parables) it contains were originally published as pamphlets, and put into book form in 1926. That it is still published almost 100 years later suggests to me the ideas it offers have stood the test of time.

Through the parables in the book, readers can see through the eyes of each story's main character mistakes being made and lessons learned. Wise choices and foolish ones. It's a way to really learn from the mistakes of others through this wonderful book.

The story I most often share when recommending the book is titled the same as the book – "The Richest Man in Babylon." In it childhood friends of Arkad (The richest man in Babylon) come to him and ask why when they all grew up together, with the same opportunities, he is the richest man in Babylon, and they are still barely making ends meet. He responds by telling them the following:

"If you have not acquired more than a bare existence in the years since we were youths, it is because you either have failed to learn the laws that govern the building of wealth, or else you do not observe them."

Ideas are helpful, but ultimately reaching YOUR financial goals will generally depend on how you "observe" – that is IMPLEMENT - any plan you create. In other words, it is not what you know, but what you DO with what you know that will make all the difference.

The author provides seven basic rules for building wealth. In my 30 plus years as a financial advisor, advising clients on wealth accumulation and investing, I have found for the majority of my fellow Americans (and probably anyone in the world), the first three rules, if followed, are the foundation of most clients I've seen who became millionaires.

1. Pay yourself first – save a part of every dollar you earn.

2. Control your expenses – money spent does not build wealth.

3. Make your money work for you by investing it wisely.

There is nothing in life that is free of risk. If you decide to invest there will be times when an investment you made loses money, especially for investments that sound "too good to be true." Should you decide to invest, a line from "The Richest Man in Babylon" might bear remembering:

"Better a little caution than a great regret."

With even a few years of careful planning and investing, one's retirement years can be greatly enhanced. The key is to ACT! The sad fact is most people don't plan to fail. But in a country I still consider the "land of opportunity," many suffer the consequences of failing to plan. The tools to be successful financially, to be able to accumulate the financial resources needed to live a comfortable, fulfilling, work-optional life are readily available to almost anyone. It is just a matter of being willing to take the time, and a total and honest look at your financial realities and what you could do to improve them to better work for you.

While neither of us can change what has happened to you in the past, you CAN use that to learn from and build on to reach the future you seek. And understanding WHY you make certain choices can be the start of CREATING the future you seek to have.

Which brings me to two important ideas to share: a quote I keep above my desk, the source unknown but obviously from someone wise, that says:

"The rich spend money on things that MAKE money; the poor spend money on things that TAKE or COST money."

Another concept I found worth thinking about is from Robert Kiyosaki's books, "Rich Dad, Poor Dad" and "Cash Flow Quadrant" about understanding what is truly an asset. I always considered a car an asset, but since it needs ongoing income to keep it, he defines it as a liability.

Q: *WHEN IS AN ASSET NOT AN ASSET?*

A: *When you have to do something you don't enjoy doing to be able to keep it.*

My goal with this book is to teach readers the "rules" for building wealth and provide ideas that can be implemented, but ultimately, your success will depend on learning the "rules" and implementing the actions and activities to enable you to achieve personal financial independence.

"Use time wisely and your chances of accumulating wealth improve dramatically.
Use money wisely and you'll be better able to afford the time to enjoy it."
(source unknown)

The Choice is Yours

While some people inherit wealth, and others may come up with an idea that makes them a millionaire or billionaire, for the majority of Americans, whether (or not) you become a (multi-) millionaire will very likely depend on the many individual CHOICES you make - the "forks" in the road of life you take which may appear minor at the time, but depending on your choices could one day mean the difference between having a truly enjoyable, fulfilling retirement, or one dependent on others for even your daily needs.

A key factor in making a wealthy choice between one or more options is understanding the longer term effects of normal, everyday CHOICES about spending, saving, investing and earning.

Often the difference between someone who faces a future of poverty, versus one who enjoys a future of prosperity are the daily CHOICES we make in our lives about:

- School
- Career /education
- Lifestyle
- Housing
- Eating
- Transportation
- Entertainment / free time (what we do for fun)
- Investing
- Shopping
- Protecting our health
- Friends

While the above categories are fairly general, following is a more detailed list of CHOICES that you are likely to be confronted with through life that can often have significant financial impact on your future:

- What you eat
- Where you shop
- Whether to invest time studying (to get better grades – and hopefully a scholarship) or not
- What courses you take in high school
- Whether to stay out of trouble or not
- What you choose for entertainment / fun
- Involvement in community activities (that can provide job referrals/work experience and possibly scholarship money)
- The friends you choose to spend time with
- Whether to smoke or not
- Whether to exercise or not (this can affect cost of health / life insurance)
- Whether to go to college, and if so, how many years, and whether full university or community college
- What to get your degree in
- What career you choose
- Whether you get a job that pays a salary, or commission
- If the company offers stock options, or provides matching dollars to a retirement plan, whether to take advantage of those programs
- If you have income, how much to spend now, and how much to save
- How and where to invest what you save
- Whether to buy a house or rent
- How much to pay for a house

- Whether to live beyond your income or not
- Whether to get a credit card, and if so, whether to pay it off every month
- Whether to have children
- If you decide to have children, how many and at what age
- If you have children, whether you continue to work
- What kind of vacations you are going to take
- Whether to get a more expensive home or expand your current home
- Whether to continue your education
- Whether to buy the "latest/greatest" in technology, or use what you have that will do the same task (at least until prices drop)
- When you marry, and whom you marry
- Whether you buy food that is already prepared or make from scratch
- Whether you spend hours a night watching TV, or get a part time job to generate income you could invest (or use to reduce debt)
- Where you shop and if you are willing to wait until what you want is on sale (even if it means you miss buying it)
- Whether to buy or lease a car (or use public transportation, such as Uber, etc.)
- If buying a car, the cost of that car (whether new or used)
- What classes you take in school
- Whether to buy something you like but don't really need (even if it's on sale)
- Whether to be an employee of someone else or have your own company
- Whether to take advantage of a company retirement plan
- And perhaps most important since believing in our ability to become rich is often a key factor in achieving it:

WHETHER YOU WANT TO BE RICH OR NOT!!!! AND IF YOU BELIEVE YOU HAVE (OR ARE IN THE PROCESS OF EARNING) THE RIGHT TO BE RICH.

Money can be your friend or foe. Will you feel bad if you are lots richer than your friends? Or your parents? If not, then doesn't it make sense to be rich. If you find you have too much to feel comfortable, you can always give it away!!

Ultimately, the key to remember is there are only three things you can actually spend in life – time, money and "talent." What you CHOOSE to do with your time, money, and talent may ultimately determine whether you are able to afford to stop working (or work only if you CHOOSE to do so) early enough in life to really enjoy it, or whether you find yourself having to get up to work for a paycheck just to afford the basic essentials in life for as long as you live.

What many people do not understand is that investing even a couple dollars a day, combined with time as your partner, can lead to far greater wealth than many realize.

While you should not save so much for the future that you don't have fun today, if you spend too much today, you may never be in a position to be able to quit working and be self-sufficient. The key is to find a balance between having fun now, but having enough money to continue to have fun without having to work to pay for it.

In other words, when confronted with different CHOICES in how to spend, save or invest your time, or your money, it is your responsibility to evaluate your options and (hopefully) make the CHOICE that will increase your potential to achieve your personal financial goals. And it is seldom too late to start if you are willing to change your lifestyle to achieve a certain goal.

Here is a case in point: Bill came to me at age 52, recently divorced with about $7,000 to his name. But he had a DREAM, and was willing to make what most would consider tough CHOICES to achieve his dream. He invested $5,000 of that $7,000, and made a commitment to invest $10,000 a year (about 25-30% of his income as I recall). By age 62, his investments had grown to $250,000 and when offered a retirement bonus, he retired. By then he had married a wonderful lady who was also a saver. Unfortunately, this client passed away at age 81, but by then, he and his wife, who earned a middle-income salary, had accumulated almost $2 million. While this may not be "normal results," it is real life proof that you could have similar potential.

Having seen this type of wealth accumulated by clients of moderate income but "wealthy mindsets," I believe anyone who truly desires to accumulate enough wealth to afford the future they seek to have, CAN DO IT!

And as one client said just the other day when we were talking about how none of her friends were saving even though she kept trying to get them to start:

> *"Many people just don't realize how EASY it is to save a couple dollars a day."*

I hope by the time you finish this book you will be better able to make informed financial CHOICEs and achieve your financial goals.

It's a matter of CHOICE!

Becoming wealthy is less about
DOING WITHOUT
than it is about MAKING CHOICES.

What's an MTE?

While **NO RETURN OR FUTURE RESULTS CAN BE GUARANTEED**, understanding the concept of wealth as a source of ongoing income can help you understand the benefits that could result by investing now and letting the funds you invest "grow" for the future.

For the purposes of this book **MTE** is my shorthand for a concept I call the (**M**)oney (**T**)ree (**E**)ffect, which I developed because many clients through the years had a difficult time visualizing their savings as an ongoing source of income.

For many years, the wealthiest people in Brevard county, FL were often those who owned citrus orchards. **They knew the secret of REAL WEALTH – a source of <u>annually renewable</u> "income."**

Their orchards produced oranges and grapefruit, year after year. All they had to do was take care of the trees, plan for forces of nature, have customers willing to pay for their product and a way to get the product to those willing to pay for it. Sadly, for many, cold temperatures killed the trees, and many orchard owners sold their land for development. Whether their "annually renewable income" continued would depend on what they did with the proceeds.

Like those citrus trees that produced "money" for their owners each year, if you save a portion of what you earn and invest it, you are essentially creating your own "money tree orchard."

Imagine an orchard of special trees that drop money on the ground. And this goes on day after day, year after year. Since the trees can only produce new money at a certain rate, the number of trees (dollars) in your orchard (portfolio) will ultimately determine how much income you will receive each year.

For a 7% MTE, the following is assumed:

- Each tree equals $100 of investments

- Each tree drops $7 a year (7% of $100)

- If you spend all the money each tree produces a year, you won't have any "seeds" to grow new trees.

- The amount of money each tree produces a year remains the same. However, if you "plant" (reinvest) some of the money your trees produce, your total number of trees, and thus the income your total orchard produces each year, should increase as well.

As with citrus orchards, an orchard (portfolio) of investments also requires proper nurturing and care. Just as weather destroyed many citrus orchards, a change in government regulations can create or destroy a business, or even an entire industry. The loss of a key executive can put an investment at risk, as can new competitors offering a new and better way to provide the same or comparable product or service. But in general, a diversified investment fund, over time, should produce annually renewable income, and require less work and expense, than orchards of citrus trees.

Throughout this book are tables of calculations. Generally, they will include a column titled "Accumulated at 7%" and another column labeled "7% MTE." The basic concept is that for each dollar you accumulate, it is assumed it will produce 7 cents (7%) a year. (See chapter titled "Why 7%")

For example, if each tree "earns" an average 7% a year, the following shows the 7% MTE based on $100 trees.

One tree ($100) will produce	$ 7 / year
10 trees ($1,000) will produce	$70 / year
100 trees ($10,000) will produce	$700 / year
1,000 trees ($100,000) will produce	$7,000 / year
And 10,000 trees ($1,000,000) will produce	$70,000 / year

In the orchard lives a cheery little elf who collects all the fallen money and gives it to you. If you spend all the money your trees produce each year, your income would remain the same. If you instead tell your elf to plant more trees (reinvest) all or some of the year's income, over time your orchard, and the income it produces, is assumed to increase.

If you CHOOSE to create your own "money tree orchard," there are a variety of money trees you can plant (i.e.: investments you can invest in: stocks, bonds, mutual funds, real estate, CD's, etc.). Some may "die" over the years, but if you have a variety of trees, you should generally get a new crop of money to spend or plant each and every year.

JUST FOR FUN: Each time you take a dollar bill of any denomination out of your wallet / purse, imagine instead of the picture in the center, there is a tree with leaves of money that could generate income year after year for the rest of your life.

WEALTH IS A CHOICE -

Seeing yourself as being worthy of being wealthy is the first step to achieving it.

Since some people have a negative view of those who are wealthy, a key question, that you must decide for yourself, is: are you TRULY **WILLING** to be wealthy?

Here might be one way to picture what wealth can provide:

Wealth **E**nables **A** **L**ife **T**ime (of) **H**appiness.

While that may not always be true, can it really hurt that much to think of wealth in those terms? Who knows .... It might just make those thoughts a reality more often than not.

Why 7%?

For many of the calculations displayed in this book, unless noted otherwise, a 7% rate of return (ROR) on the monies being invested is assumed.

While it's likely true if you want your money in safe, principal always protected investments that a high rate of return is unlikely, between 1975 and 2014, the annualized annual return of the Lipper Balanced Fund Index (an equally weighted index of the 30 largest U.S. balanced funds) averaged over 10%.

Suppose we assume an average return of 8% on stocks, 5% on bonds, and 2% on cash investments. That means if each $100 in your portfolio is invested as follows:

$70 invested in stocks (at 8% would generate $5.60 / year)

$20 invested in bonds (at 5% would generate $ 1.00 / year)

$10 invested in cash (at 2% would generate $0.20 / year)

The total return on $100 would be $6.80 (6.8%). Rounded to the nearest whole percent, that would be a total return of 7% a year.

<u>REMEMBER: 7% IS NOT A GUARANTEED RETURN.</u>
For calculations using other rates, tables in the appendix provide rates of 0-8% that you can use for your own calculations.

The Freedom to Say "No"

Money, even lots of it, doesn't necessarily buy happiness. When you consider people like Steve Jobs, who was worth billions but still died at a young age, it can't even always buy good health.

And it can't buy REAL friends.

I don't remember the exact year I read this, but it was after the movie "Crocodile Dundee" hit big and Paul Hogan suddenly had megabucks.

In an interview he was asked what all this popularity and money had brought him. His response stuck in my mind all these years because it is SOOOOO true of people for whom money is a tool instead of their master.

What he said was that having money gave him the freedom to say "no" to scripts he doesn't like or work he doesn't want to do. It allowed him the freedom to really CHOOSE what to do with his time, and his talents.

> ***The key is not just wealth accumulation,***
> ***but at an age you can enjoy it.***
> *How much in "passive" (wealth generated) income,*
> *would you need to feel you are truly confident*
> *of being able to finance your income needs*
> *for the rest of your life?*

All You Really Need to Know to Become a Millionaire

As simplistic as it might seem, all you need to KNOW to become a millionaire is really quite simple:

1. The number of years you have to achieve that million dollar goal.
2. The amount of money you already have available that can be used toward achieving that million dollar goal.
3. The assumed rate of return, preferably a net after tax return, that you REALISTICALLY expect the funds referenced in #2 to earn – per year - during the accumulation period.
4. The percent per year you REALISTICALLY expect to increase your annual investments.
5. The average rate of return you REALISTICALLY expect annual investments to earn per year.

With the above values, you have the information needed to calculate whether you are already on track to accumulate a million dollars without needing to make additional investments, or to calculate how much you would need to invest starting now if you increase the investment amount by the rate you specified in #4.

For example, suppose your goal is to accumulate $1 million in 30 years. In addition:

1. You have $100,000 already saved toward that goal.
2. You assume the $100,000 earns 5% / year net of taxes.

Using Table FVS-1 in Appendix A, find the value where 30 years and 5% intersect. That "future value multiplier" is $4,322. Since the values in the table assume an initial investment of $1,000, to calculate the "investment multiplier" you would divide $100,000 by $1,000 =

100. To calculate what your current $100,000 would be worth in 30 years, multiply the "future value multiplier ($4,322) by the "investment multiplier" (100). Result: $432,200.

That means you'll need an additional $567,800 to have $1 million. To calculate the annual investments needed, assume the following:

3. You will increase your annual investment 3% each year.

4. These annual investments will earn, net of taxes, 6% / year.

Using Table IIA-3 in Appendix F, you would again use the 30 year column, but since the assumed investment rate is 6%, the 6% row is used (note: the 3% AIIPY in the upper left corner of this table represents: 3% Annual Investment Increase Per Year)

The value in this table is used as a divisor. To calculate the initial annual investment needed to accumulate the remaining $567,800, divide that amount by the value where 30 years and 6% intersect. That value is 110.54, so you would divide $567,800 by 110.5. The result: $5,136.60 (rounded to $5,137)).

That means the first year you would need to invest $5,137, and each year increase the amount invested by 3% (so in year 2 it would be $5,290, in year 3 it would be $5,449, and so on)

The "Path to a Million" table "proves" these calculations (values are slightly different than calculated using the Appendix due to rounding):

PATH TO A MILLION

a) Year	b) Current investment	c) Future value at 5% a year	d) Additional amount invested	e) Future value at 6% a year	f) Total account value
1	$100,000	$105,000	$5,137	$5,137	$110,137
2		$110,250	$5,291	$10,736	$120,986
3		$115,763	$5,450	$16,830	$132,593
4		$121,551	$5,613	$23,454	$145,004
5		$127,628	$5,782	$30,642	$158,271
.....					
10		$162,889	$6,703	$76,530	$239,419
.....					
20		$265,330	$9,008	$239,902	$505,232
.....					
29		$411,614	$11,753	$524,286	$935,900
30		$432,194	$12,106	$567,849	$1,000,043

The following provides an explanation of each column above:

a) Year = the years into the future from when you start.

b) Current investment = $100,000.

c) Future value of a rate of return (ROR) of 5%.

d) Starting with the initial annual investment needed ($5,137 a year), the investment amount is increased 3% / year.

e) The cumulative future value of annual investments assuming a 6% / year return.

f) Shows the total of b) and e), the accumulating value of the initial $100,000 investment plus annual investments.

While the above calculations may seem like a lot of math, particularly if you don't enjoy that subject, by using the tables, all you will need to do is some simple addition, subtraction, multiplication, or division.

You now have learned what you need to know to become a millionaire, and how to use that information to do the necessary calculations to see if you need additional investments, and if so, how much.

Knowing is important, but DOING is what is needed to turn a wish into "done."

Will you use this knowledge to make being a millionaire (or more) a reality?

The CHOICE is yours.

You don't have to begin rich to become rich.

Unfashionably Rich

Interviewing dozens of millionaires who responded to his survey in 1995–1996, Dr. Thomas Stanley, ("The Millionaire Next Door," and "The Millionaire Mind") found a large majority were first generation millionaires, and only a small minority attended a private school. Asked about buying habits, the typical millionaire (*and most were multi-millionaires*) told him they never spent more than $399 for a suit, $140 for a pair of shoes, or $235 for a watch. In other words, celebrities who sell clothing, perfumes, and other stuff didn't get much business from these millionaires.

Which leads me to the picture shown above.

Often when a product is endorsed or produced by someone "famous," it costs more than a similar, or better, equivalent. Which means buying a "designer / celebrity" item is making someone else richer instead of you.

A simple example is clothing. You can get as much use from a generic pair of jeans as buying the celebrity / designer version.

Of course, it's fun to buy new things, look nice and get complimented on your new purchases. And if you buy at thrift stores and consignment shops friends might not be as impressed (*It drives my mom crazy that I shop in thrift stores.*), but what if buying "generic" or at thrift stores, even for a few years, meant hundreds or thousands of dollars of extra income a year in the future. Income that you could spend, or that could enable you to retire sooner.

There are four different brands of jeans in the picture above: *AZI, Guess, Coldwater Creek*, and *Boyfriend*. And they are all different. But three of the four pairs have something very important in common. Can you guess what that is?

Not sure? Here's the answer: three of the four jeans cost $3-$5 each (for a total of $12.00) and one pair cost $132.00. Which means of the jeans pictured, one pair cost over $100 **more** than the other three COMBINED. *Can you tell which one is the $132.00 pair?*

The same idea applies to other things - from tee shirts to business suits to evening gowns to beaded jackets to furniture to cars. And it's not just for women – My boyfriend has name brand running shorts, sweaters, a beautiful suede jacket, and the tuxedo he wears to black tie functions we attend is one I bought at a thrift store for a fraction of what he would have paid new.

The bottom line is after one washing, it's unlikely even an expert could tell if an item of clothing was purchased new, or at a thrift or consignment store.

This same idea applies to activities such as concerts and sports events. Assuming the cost of attending a live sports event adds up to $100 with tickets, food, beverages and parking fees, the savings from watching the event at home for one season could be enough to buy a big screen TV for watching future events, and have money left to invite friends over to watch it together and have a nice spread of food and beverages all paid for from the savings that added to YOUR wealth instead of someone else's.

The following "Unfashionable Rich" table shows how much you could accumulate investing $500 a year at 7% for just five years, and then let it grow.

In addition, if at any time, you decided to stop reinvesting the earnings and start withdrawing what the money accumulated by that year earned, again assuming an annual return of 7%, the "7% MTE" column shows how much you could take out each year, "forever." ***NOTE: Once you start taking out the earnings, the accumulated value would stop increasing.***

UNFASHIONABLY RICH

Year	Invested	Accumulated at 7%	*MTE at 7%
1	$500	$500	
2	$500	$1,035	
3	$500	$1,607	
4	$500	$2,220	
5	$500	$2,875	
6		$3,077	$215
7		$3,292	$230
8		$3,522	$247
9		$3,769	$264
10		$4,033	$282
:::::			
15		$5,656	$396
:::::			
20		$7,933	$555
:::::			
25		$11,127	$779
::::			
30		$15,606	$1,092

*MTE = **M**oney **T**ree **E**ffect (see chapter "What's an MTE?")

So the question to ask yourself: Do you want to be the person who spends $1000 a year on new clothes, or be the person who spends $500 a year on the same basic wardrobe and invests the $500 they didn't spend to add fuel to their personal wealth machine?

The CHOICE is yours.

Why are YOU Going to a Personal Trainer?

That was the question I asked my mom one Christmas.

As usual, the family was together for Christmas, and I commented to my 75-year-old mother how great she looked. She told me she had hired a personal trainer.

Since I knew mom walked the beach at least a mile most days, and went to the gym as well, I asked her why she felt she needed a personal trainer. Her response really made me think about what she said in relation to building wealth.

Here is what she said: *"Yes, I walked the beach, and even went to the gym, but when I got tired of a particular machine, I quit and went to another, so I never really got the benefit of any of the machines I was using, or the time I was spending at the gym."*

She said with the personal trainer, she had someone making her stick to her routine so she really got RESULTS.

By the way, mom is now 93 years old, and weather permitting, still tries to walk a mile every morning around her apartment complex, and still lives on – and walks up to and down from - her 2nd floor apartment. About her only concession to age is buying bottled water in packs of 6 instead of 24 so she can carry them up on her own.

What I have seen in over 30 years working with clients is similar accountability toward "exercising investing" works as well.

When an automatic investment program is used, many investors forget they are investing because in their mind, the money is no longer available. I doubt more than 10 clients have, ON THEIR OWN, voluntarily increased their investment. But through the years, with some nagging from me, some agreed to go up $10, $25, or even $50 a month. Most refused, but those who did increase by even small amounts each year, really saw a difference.

Consider this hypothetical example: Joe invests $50 a month. Sue invests $50 a month to start, but each year she increases her investments by JUST $100 a year – less than $3 a day.

While no job or business guarantees increased income, the "Small Increases" table below assumes an initial annual income of $20,000, increasing 3% a year over the 40 years illustrated. By year 40, Joe is still investing only $600 a year (less than 1% of his income), while Sue is investing $4,500 in year 40, about 7% of her total income.

SMALL INCREASES PRODUCE NICE RESULTS.

Year	Assumed income 3% increase	Joe's investment	Joe's accumulated wealth	Sue's investment	Sue's accumulated wealth
1	$20,000	$600	$600	$600	$600
2	$20,600	$600	$1,242	$700	$1,342
3	$21,218	$600	$1,929	$800	$2,236
4	$21,855	$600	$2,664	$900	$3,292
5	$22,510	$600	$3,450	$1,000	$4,523
.....					
10	$26,095	$600	$8,290	$1,500	$13,742
.....					
20	$35,070	$600	$24,597	$2,500	$54,591
.....					
30	$47,131	$600	$56,676	$3,500	$148,763
.....					
40	$63,341	$600	$119,781	$4,500	$347,831
TOTAL	INVESTED	$24,000		$102,000	

Over that 40 years, Joe invested a total of $24,000. Sue a total of $102,000. A $78,000 difference. But there is also a difference in wealth - Sue's extra investments result in accumulated wealth of over $228,000 more than Joe.

BENEFITING FROM ACCOUNTABILITY

According to a study by Gail Matthews, a psychology professor at Dominican University referenced in an article in the March 2015 issue of Money magazine,

- You're significantly more likely to achieve your aims just by writing them down.
- Those sharing goals with a friend via weekly updates achieved their aims significantly more often than those who didn't.

Change the Chairs

I just LOVE this story.

Whether or not you like Donald Trump from a political perspective, I find every time I read one of his books I get at least one good idea, and usually more, that I can apply in my own life or that could help a client in theirs.

This story wasn't actually from Trump, but from Kim Kiyosaki, wife of Robert "Rich Dad, Poor Dad" Kiyosaki and was titled "A Tale of Two Solutions."

You can read the whole story by Googling "A Tale of Two Solutions," but here is a summary:

She and Robert had been invited by Mr. Trump to visit him at Trump National Golf Club in L.A., and as they were taking a tour of the club, he told them a story.

When he bought the club, it was losing money because the main ballroom could only seat 150 people, so they couldn't compete with other clubs for many of the larger events.

What she calls the "obvious" solution was to build an addition. The estimated cost was $3 million, and it would take six to nine months to complete.

As her story goes, one evening Mr. Trump stopped to observe a party in the ballroom and noticed an older woman struggling to get out of her very nice, but big and heavy, chair.

That observation led to a less obvious solution: Mr. Trump had his team do some research and found he could increase seating to 250 people using smaller chairs. Which is what he did.

On top of that, he sold the big, heavy chairs and instead of costing him money to be able to seat more people in the ballroom, he actually made money on the deal.

And it wasn't just the $3 million he didn't have to spend, or the money he made selling the old chairs that he profited from. For the six - nine months it would have taken to build the addition, even assuming the addition was totally separate and didn't interfere with use of the existing ballroom, by having 100 extra seats to use during those six - nine months, he could compete for more events. Suppose each week he had 100 extra guests dining at the club. And further suppose each of those extra guests created a net profit of $10. That would be $1,000 a week. With an average 4.3 weeks per month, and assuming the renovation that now wasn't needed would have taken seven months, that would be roughly 30 weeks, or $30,000 of additional profit the club was able to make by having the extra seating available for seven months.

While that may be pocket change to Donald Trump, it's still real money that could be spent on other things he might enjoy more than watching his club getting an addition - donating to a local charity he supported, offering $30,000 in gift cards to organizations to buy needed supplies, or many other uses that could benefit him, his club, or organizations he supported.

Could you find similar "solutions" for how you do things in your own life that could be a source of increased wealth for you? A good place to start is by creating a budget to see where you are spending money now, or looking at things you might be planning to spend money on that could be accomplished in a "wealthier" way.

"Man can alter his life by altering his thinking."
– William James

"The eye sees only what the mind is prepared to comprehend."
– Henri-Louis Bergson

"No problem can be solved by the same consciousness that created it. We need to see the world anew."
– Albert Einstein

From Zero to Half a Million in 10 Years

A young salesman came to my office in 1999. Asked what I did, I told him I help clients accumulate wealth so they can tell their boss to "give the job to someone who really NEEDS it."

He expected to earn $50,000 the following year, and $100,000 within four years. He was single with minimal expenses. He enjoyed his job but it wasn't his desired career. His goal was to be able to take time off to sail, start a family, and maybe start a business.

We decided to create a hypothetical plan with him initially spending $36,000 of the $50,000, and investing the rest assuming:

- 7% rate of return on the monies invested
- An increase in spending of 4% / year
- Income starting at $50,000 at age 26 and increasing 12% / year through year eight, then leveling off in years nine and ten.

Whether he actually achieves his income goals, the calculations make for an interesting 10-year plan. As you can see, his annual investment was projected to increase from $14,000 a year to almost $60,000 a year, yet he was spending more each year as well.

ZERO TO HALF A MILLION

Age	Income	Taxes and spending	Invested	Accumulated at 7%
26	$50,000	$36,000	$14,000	$14,000
27	$56,000	$37,440	$18,560	$33,540
28	$62,720	$38,938	$23,782	$59,670
29	$70,246	$40,495	$29,751	$93,598
30	$78,676	$42,115	$36,561	$136,711
31	$88,117	$43,800	$44,318	$190,599
32	$98,691	$45,551	$53,140	$257,080
33	$110,534	$47,374	$63,161	$338,236
34	$110,534	$49,268	$61,266	$423,179
35	$110,534	$51,239	$59,295	$512,096

Now, just for fun, let's take this plan one step further. Suppose at 35 he decided to get married, spend 100% of his "job" income, but leave the $512,096 invested and it earned 7% a year.

Using Table FVS-1 in Appendix A, calculate how much those funds would be worth if the investment continued to earn 7% a year and he reinvested the earnings.

Answer: In 10 years (at 45) it would be worth $1,007,293.
In 20 years (at 55) it would be worth $1,981,811.

Even taking inflation into account, the income the accumulated savings could generate is not a bad trade-off for 10 years of living on less than he earned.

FROM MIDDLE INCOME TO MILLIONAIRE

I was recently asked my thoughts about whether I thought those with middle quintile incomes could become millionaires, and if so, what traits I thought were important. Here was my response:

1. They have patience. They look beyond instant gratification to potential future gratification.
2. They understand how time and compound interest can help them accumulate wealth.
3. They value who they ARE more than what others think they SHOULD be.
4. They have taken time to understand investing so they are better able to make more informed financial choices.
5. They think in terms of money as a tool to achieve their long term financial goals, not just as something available to spend.

Financial Truths

The following are from the outline of a financial seminar I offered over 30 years ago that seem as relevant today as they did back then:

1. **There is no such thing as a universal portfolio.**
2. **Investments are not made in a vacuum.**
3. **A guarantee is only as good as the guarantor.**
4. **No rearrangement of bad eggs will make a good omelet.**
5. **T.A.N.S.T.A.A.F.L.***
6. **There are no dumb questions when it comes to YOUR money.**

There Ain't No Such Thing As A Free Lunch!

Financial Self Defense

My local Chamber of Commerce had a seminar titled "Self Defense through Mental Preparedness" presented by our local sheriff that encouraged us to focus on:

- Being AWARE of our surroundings at all times.

- Having an "exit plan" should someone start shooting.

- (As best as we can) create a "safe environment" in your home and workplace.

It was an excellent presentation and something each of us would be wise to implement. A similar "mental preparedness" concept could be useful in building wealth by:

- Being aware of where the money you receive / earn both comes from, and where it goes.

- Having a clear financial goal, both in what it is, and what it is likely to cost.

- Creating a plan to turn habits that reduce your wealth into ones that increase it.

It can help to keep in mind a comment in "Faster, Cheaper, Better" by Michael Hammer and Lisa Hershman: "If you can't measure it, you can't improve it."

I encourage clients to make saving / investing both easy, and habit, to build wealth by setting up a systematic investment plan. Even if it's just $30 a month (the equivalent of $1 a day), it's a start, and what most clients found after the first couple months is they didn't miss it and were able to increase their monthly investment through the years.

SAVINGS = a source of future spending

Book Review:

THE HAPPINESS ADVANTAGE

by Shawn Achor

Psychologists call what happens when the brain acts on what it THINKS will happen "Expectancy Theory." The belief is that expecting positive outcomes make them more likely to arrive, and priming yourself to expect a positive outcome increases your chances of seeing it.

The book mentions a video of teams – one in white shirts, one in black shirts – playing basketball. Viewers are told to count how many times the white team passed the ball. Shortly into the video, a person in a gorilla suit walks across the court. Almost no one saw the gorilla – they saw what they were told to look for.

Opportunity often comes knocking, but we are often too busy to open the door. Are you focused on what it takes to reach your goals? If not, could refocusing help you make more choices that enhance your likelihood of achieving YOUR goal.

One of the suggestions from the book: Start looking for positive experiences and keep a journal of those experiences.

FOUR STEPS TO ACHIEVING A GOAL

1. **Be in the right place at the right time.**
2. **Recognize an opportunity when it is presented.**
3. **Be able, financial and emotionally, to take advantage of the opportunity when it is presented.**
4. **TAKE ACTION – Remember, opportunity may knock, but YOU must open the door.**

"I Can't Afford to Save"

One of the things that has changed little in the more than 30 years I've been a financial professional is that the same people who can "afford" a new car every three to four years, who spend thousands a year on vacations, buy new wardrobes for a special occasion, or go out to dinner every night ... "can't" seem to find $100 / month (less than $5 a day) to invest for their future.

I've heard many "excuses" through the years on why someone "can't afford to invest."

COMMON EXCUSES FOR NOT SAVING NOW

- It's too late for me to start.
- I have children to put through college first.
- I have enough now.
- I'll be different than those other retirees who have no money.
- My company has a pension plan.
- I don't understand investments / investing is too confusing.
- My children will take care of me.
- I plan to work until I die.
- Everyone is trying to rip you off.
- I can't afford to save.
- I don't have time.

And last but not least .... "I'LL HIT THE LOTTERY."

But I haven't heard many really valid ***REASONS***.

If you have not started investing on a regular basis, my question to you is "why?" And to your response I would likely ask: "Is that REALLY, REALLY TRUE?"

In his book, "Excuses Begone!" by Dr. Wayne W. Dyer concludes that often the difference between achieving a goal and not doing so comes down to your BELIEFS. So I would pose the following questions to you, with the goal of being wealthy (whatever your definition of that might be):

- Do you BELIEVE that while acting with honesty, integrity and fairness, you have the CAPABILITY within you to become (financially) wealthy?
- Do you BELIEVE you have the ATTITUDE within you to be WILLING TO BE (financially) wealthy?
- Do you BELIEVE that you WANT to not just become, but ***BE*** (financially) wealthy?
- Do you BELIEVE that having (financial) wealth is an opportunity to do good for you and those whose wellbeing is of importance to you?
- Do you BELIEVE that virtually any choice / decision you make in life may be leading you toward, or away from, becoming (financially) wealthy?

If you can answer "YES" to all the above, then you have taken the first steps to becoming financially wealthy.

The next step is to understand, and passionately BELIEVE, the following is true:

There is no really good REASON (although there are lots of great EXCUSES) that someone should not have created a substantial investment portfolio over a 20–40 year period of time.

Ultimately, accumulating financial wealth is about converting a portion of each dollar you earn into future wealth. And a key tool to accomplish that is to realize how even small changes in spending and investing habits can produce long term wealth.

Make enhancing your long term wealth a daily HABIT. Before you invest time or money in something, really think about whether what you plan to do will help you in reaching your desired future goal.

How to Become a Millionaire

If you ask an typical American their financial goal, many will say they want to (at least) be a millionaire.

The reality is that to become a millionaire, you basically need to do as Arkad told his friends in the book the "The Richest Man in Babylon" by George S. Clason.

In the book, Arkad, considered to be the "richest man" in the city of Babylon, is asked by friends he grew up with what amounts to: "why are you so rich and we are not." His response to them:

"If you have not acquired more than a bare existence in the years since we were youths, it is because you either have failed to learn the laws that govern the building of wealth, or else you do not observe them."

As simplistic as that sounds, the essence of what it takes to become a millionaire can be found in these 3 basic principles:

1. Pay yourself first.
2. Control your Expenses.
3. Put your savings to work.

I often find once someone starts saving a portion of their income and realizes how easy it is, it also becomes easier to control their expenses and save more. As for putting those savings to work, the rate of return investments earn IS important in the overall process as you can see by the following tables that illustrate various "paths to a million," but the real key is to start!!

PATH TO A MILLION: SINGLE LUMP SUM NEEDED
(value to nearest $1,000)

Years to accumulate	Assumed annual investment return			
	2%	4%	6%	8%
40	$453,000	$208,000	$97,000	$46,000
35	$500,000	$253,000	$130,000	$68,000
30	$552,000	$308,000	$174,000	$100,000
25	$610,000	$375,000	$233,000	$146,000
20	$673,000	$456,000	$312,000	$215,000
15	$743,000	$555,000	$417,000	$315,000
10	$820,000	$676,000	$558,000	$463,000
5	$906,000	$822,000	$747,000	$681,000

PATH TO A MILLION: Investing a FIXED ANNUAL amount
(rounded to nearest $100)

Years to accumulate	Assumed annual investment return			
	2%	4%	6%	8%
40	$16,600	$10,500	$6,500	$3,900
35	$20,000	$13,600	$9,000	$5,800
30	$24,600	$17,800	$12,600	$8,800
25	$31,200	$24,000	$18,200	$13,700
20	$41,200	$33,600	$27,200	$21,900
15	$57,800	$49,900	$43,000	$58,300
10	$91,300	$83,300	$75,900	$69,000
5	$192,200	$184,600	$177,400	$170,400

NOTE: Tables in Appendix F provide the values to calculate initial investment amount if you plan to increase annual investments by 1, 3, or 5 percent.

While accumulating a million dollars is a worthy goal achieved by only a small percentage of U.S. families, it is important to understand even that may not be enough for many to be truly financially independent.

For example, suppose you have a million dollars and want it to provide income for 30 years. The "30 years of income – initial withdrawal" table illustrates the amount you could withdraw the first year if the income over

30 years was to remain flat, versus if you wanted to withdraw 3% more each of those years.

30 YEARS OF INCOME – INITIAL WITHDRAWAL

ROR*	Fixed withdrawal	3% increasing withdrawal
5%	$61,954	$43,449
6%	$68,537	$49,017

*ROR = rate of return

As you can see, even small difference can add up over time, so careful planning in advance could mean the difference between having several thousand more, or less, a year to spend, or running out of money while you still have years that income is needed.

PUTTING A MILLION IN PERSPECTIVE

- A million seconds = 278 hours = less than 12 days.
- A million pennies = $10,000.
- A million feet = 190 miles.
- A million dollars earning 7% is enough to generate $70,000 a year "forever."

Teach Your Children Well

Do you spend less than you earn and invest the rest? Do you talk about money with your children? Are you teaching your children about investing and saving while they are young?

One of the sadder and difficult situations I've had to deal with as a financial adviser is when parents destroy their own chance at financial independence bailing their children out of bad choices. I know they love their children and believe they are doing what is best, but they may actually be harming both their own ability, and their child's, to become financially able to afford the lifestyle they each seek to have.

I was meeting with a young man who had saved since he was a kid, but he couldn't get his 10-year-old daughter to save even part of her birthday money. He tried to explain to her that if she saved some of it now, she would have more to spend later when she might find something she really wanted. Her response was classic 10 year old: "but I have you, dad."

In addition to the "car" story I shared in "My Own Story," I shared with him some of the other ideas I learned from mom and dad or proposed to clients through the years to help them better prepare their children for the real world where the "bank of mom and dad" might not be open. He wrote several down and said he was going to give them a try with his daughter, and that he wanted a copy of my book as soon as I was done.

Here are some ideas if you have children and/or grandchildren that might need a little help becoming better managers of their money:

1. BOSS DAY. Mom and dad started this when I was about nine. The weekend or two after our respective birthdays, my brother, sister and I were allowed to be "boss for the day." We got to choose where to go eat, what to do for the day, with the only prohibition that we could

not use our "power" to hurt each other (such as making one of them stay home while we went out). It was a good lesson in not using power to hurt others.

2. FINE FOR LEAVING THE LIGHTS ON. It's been more than 50 years, but I still remember having 25 cents taken out of my allowance for each time I left the lights on in a room I had left. Dad said if I wanted to waste money, it was coming out of my pocket. It may sound cruel, but in the real world, wasting now may result in wanting later. And to this day, I regularly turn out the lights when I leave a room.

3. EXTRA EARNINGS. My brother gave his kids an allowance of $1 for each year of their age (so at 10, my nephew had an allowance of $10 / month). One day we were sitting around and my nephew was complaining that his friend got $20 a month, but upon further questioning, it turned out my nephew had over $600 in savings. When I asked him where that came from, he said his dad paid him to do extra chores. At 10 he may not have understood the valuable lesson he was learning about work and pay, but what a great way to prepare someone for being a success in the real world.

4. FAMILY 401k PLAN. I've found many otherwise intelligent people tell me the reason they didn't invest above a certain amount in their company retirement plan is because the company only matched a certain percent. In my opinion not a smart financial choice, particularly if they had funds available to invest, but something that often happens. Anyway, one of the things I've suggested parents create is a "Family 401K Plan" to encourage their children, even into early adulthood, to save for the future. Usually, I suggest it when a teenager gets a job and is earning at least a couple hundred dollars a month. The idea is simple. If the child agrees to invest $50 / month from their earnings, mom and dad will match it with $50 – HOWEVER, the deal is if they want to take money out within a year, the first money that comes out is what was put in by mom and dad. I also suggest that to get the child in the habit of increasing the amount invested, to start with $50/$50 split, but each year increase the child's contribution and decrease the parent's contribution by $10 a month.

5. LIVING ON A BUDGET. This idea actually came from a 13 year old. She wanted a pager. Her parents said "no." They came to me. I thought it a FABULOUS idea, so the daughter drew up a budget that included things like the monthly pager bill, going out with friends to the movies, snacks from the school vending machines, attending school events, and so on. If she ran out of money before the end of the month, she could do things with her parents, but she didn't get more money. The first month was tough since she hadn't budgeted for the pager deposit, and for the first couple months she ran out of money before the end of the month and if she wanted to go out to the movies or such, she had to go with her parents, but when she was older, she said it had been a great lesson.

6. DESIGNER VERSUS STORE BRAND. Often kids want the designer brand of shoes, clothes, and such that cost far more than the store brand but serve the same purpose. I encourage parents to tell the child that they (the parents) will pay the amount of the store brand, but the child will have to use his/her own money to pay the difference if they want to buy the designer brand. I'm told many children decide the store brand will work just fine.

7. A WISE FATHER. Some years ago I was dating a very wealthy man. Knowing I was a financial advisor, he shared a story I've shared with clients for years. His daughter wanted a car. He could easily afford to buy it for her, but that would not teach her anything. He offered to buy her the car, but she had to make payments (no interest) to him until it was paid for. But in the meantime, he invested each payment she made. When she made her final payment, he gave her the statement for the account he had set up for her. A great lesson on how regular "payments" can add up.

My dad believed we children had the ability to do whatever we set our minds to, as long as we were willing to work to make it happen. He also believed strongly in personal responsibility.

I did get a car about a year after I tried to get him to buy me one, and it was one I was proud to own because I bought it with money I EARNED. A lesson it took a while to appreciate, but a valuable one.

If you have children, I strongly encourage you to read "The Millionaire Next Door" to understand the difference between being "Income Affluent," and "Balance Sheet Affluent." It could help you and your children work together so you all become financially independent.

And by the way, if you have children that move back in after they start working, it is NOT cruel to charge them rent. Once a person is earning money, they need to understand what they want generally has a cost, and you can always invest the money and give it to them at a later date.

DON'T JUST EXPLAIN THINGS – TELL THEM WHY IT MATTERS.

Test Your Financial Knowledge

There are numerous "financial literacy" tests available on the internet, but I found few of the questions they ask pertain to wealth accumulation or how to calculate what one would need in financial resources to finance a desired level of income from investments.

The following questions are designed to test your knowledge of some very basic rules regarding achieving ***your*** long term financial goals. Answers are at the bottom of the page.

You should not feel bad, or foolish, if you don't know the answers. Various surveys suggest most Americans, even those not many years from when they would like to stop working, are not able to answer these questions. The positive difference between you and many other Americans is the information in this book provides the tools needed to answer these questions:

1. If the cost of living increased at 4% a year, 36 years from now, how much would you need to afford a lifestyle that costs $1,000 in current dollars?
2. If your investments earn 5% a year, how much would you need to invest to be able to withdraw $10,000 a year without using any of your principal?
3. If your investments earn 5% a year, to have $1 million accumulated in 40 years, how much would you need to invest each year?
4. If a tax free investment earns 5%, and you are in the 25% tax bracket, what taxable rate would you need to earn to equal 5% after taxes?
5. What is the main reason most individuals do not accumulate enough wealth (financial resources) to finance their desired lifestyle during their post-work years?

ANSWERS:

1) $4,000. Clue: The rule of 72, which says if you divide the assumed rate (4) into 72, the answer is the number of years (18) it would take the initial amount ($1,000) to double. Since 36 / 18 = 2, that means the $1,000 initial amount would double twice - $1,000 > $2,000 > $4,000.

2) $200,000. Clue: The formula for calculating how much you would need to invest to generate a certain amount of annual income is: Annual income to be generated ($10,000) divided by the assumed rate of return as a decimal (.05) = $200,000.

3) $8,278. Clue: This is a little more complicated, but in the appendix you will find Table IIA-0, which provides data to calculate the initial annual investment needed to accumulate a specified amount. Using that table, you would use the applicable year column (40), and the applicable row (5%). The value where the 5% row and 40 year column intersect is 120.8. If you divide the future goal ($1,000,000) by 120.8, the result is $8,278. This is the annual amount you would need to invest to have $1 million in 40 years assuming your investments earned 5% a year.

4) 6.67%. Clue: If the tax rate is 25%, then you would only get to keep 75% of the taxable rate. The initial formula would be 75% of "what rate" = 5%. If you divide the tax-free rate (5) by the amount that you would get to keep (.75) the result is 6.67%. To confirm that, you can multiply 6.67% by 25% (.25). Answer: 1.67%. That is the percent that would be paid in taxes, leaving 5% AFTER tax as the return.

5) There are a number of reasons, but I think at the top of the list are a) procrastination, and b) not knowing how to determine if you are on track.

Giving the Gift of Wealth

When Bobby and I shared our first Christmas, along with a pair of fluffy "dog" slippers, he gave me a beautiful gold necklace. You can probably imagine his surprise when I asked him to return it.

My reason was simple: I had a drawer of gold jewelry I seldom wore anymore. Years before, when I thought it important to LOOK rich rather than BE rich, I regularly wore 7- 8 gold necklaces at a time. I still have a couple that have real meaning to me, but the others I sold and invested the proceeds in income producing investments.

I believe many adults will agree that if there is something they really want, they'll buy it themselves, and too much of Christmas gifting has become something we do because it's "expected."

For birthdays, we generally go to dinner with friends, and if they want to give us a gift, we ask them to donate money or food to the SPCA. For Christmas, we "gift" ourselves a trip. We've had a lot of fun, lots of memories, and no more stuff that needed to be stored or "displayed" somewhere.

With my immediate family, once the "kids" knew where "Santa" gifts really came from, for Christmas we tried different things. Kids bought gifts for parents and parents for their kids, but otherwise we each pulled a name and bought a gift for one other person. We tried the "Chinese Auction" idea but that got tiresome. For a couple years those who wanted to participate each put $20 and their name and chosen charity (even if it was the "charity of self") in for a "charity raffle." Whoever's name was drawn got the money.

It was a win-win way to enjoy the real spirit of the holiday and have more time to spend enjoying our time together.

When you have all you really need, helping others can be the most fun gift of all.

Take Hwy 70-20-10 From Debt to Greater Wealth

A quote I've had in my office for years says: "*When you are dependent on someone else for your daily needs, you better keep them happy.*"

This chapter is for readers who have outstanding debt other than a mortgage payment or a vehicle with an interest rate below what can be earned on a reasonably-safe investment.

A chapter in "The Richest Man in Babylon" tells of a man in ancient Babylon so deep in debt he left his wife with her father and left town to seek easy wealth elsewhere. He ended up a slave, but in the process received advice that enabled him to eliminate his debt and become "a man of means worthy of respect in (his) native city," and how a professor helping translate the Babylonian tablets used the same ideas to help himself and his wife get out of the debt and restore their credit.

This story led to what I call my "70-20-10 Plan." The idea is really simple. If you have debt, until the debt is eliminated, you would:

- Live on 70% of your income (even if it means getting part time work, or renting out a room, etc. to increase income if available spending cuts are too limited).

- Use 20% of income to pay off debt.

- Save 10% (psychologically, this gives you the opportunity to move FORWARD financially, not just be focused on fixing the past).

I realize it's not easy to suddenly live on 70% of your actual income – particularly if you had been spending more than you earn for years and likely already have lots of built-in expenses. But it is doable IF, and "IF" is the key, you want to go from being in debt to building serious wealth.

The first place to start is to not look at it as a sacrifice, but as a wonderful opportunity to be proud of being free of debt. To know each dollar you earn (other than perhaps a mortgage), is going to build a better life for you and your loved ones instead of some lender.

MAKE IT AN ADVENTURE!!! Examine how you spent money in the past, and see if you can find ways to achieve similar benefits, but at lower cost.

Incidentally, the order in which you pay down debt can increase or decrease the amount of time it takes to eliminate it. This is my suggestion:

1. List your credit cards in order of interest rate, lowest to highest.

2. Within each interest rate, list in order of largest to smallest.

3. Pay the minimum on all but the bottom (highest rate) card. Then with whatever you can afford, pay all the interest PLUS at least 2% of the balance on the card with the highest rate and the smallest balance.

4. When a card is paid off, take 10% of what you had been paying monthly and treat yourself to something you enjoy.

5. REPEAT.

The beauty of this idea is that once you pay off your debt, you now have 20% of your income to apply toward increased spending or building wealth. If you worked extra hours to meet your spending / saving / debt payment needs, now you could stop.

The CHOICE is yours, but if you now have "stress level debt," this idea could help both your wallet and your health.

A Year in "Poverty"....?

This is much easier to consider when you are just getting out of school, don't yet have others dependent on you, and are not already locked into payments for debts already accumulated, but please don't let that stop you from at least "doing the numbers." You might be surprised.

Maybe I'm fortunate I came of age before credit cards were widespread, and obtaining credit by someone without a reliable source of income was very rare as well.

The result was as I was looking to buy my first car (in 1971), as much as I wanted a Dodge Challenger, at $3,000 it was way out of my budget, while a used Mustang was only $750. This turned out to be one of my wiser moves, though not by CHOICE, since at the time, if I could have qualified for a loan, I probably would have bought the Challenger. While I admit I didn't think in those terms at the time, here is the math:

Not counting taxes or interest I would have paid if I had borrowed money to buy the car, I saved $2,250 when I was 21.

The table below takes values from Table FVS-1 in Appendix A. The value in the column titled "45" is the average of the values for 40 and 50 years. Since these values are based on an investment of $1,000, and the amount of savings on the car is $2,250, the "investment multiplier" would be $2,250 / $1,000 = 2.25. The value in the column titled "x 2.25" is an estimate of what $2,250 invested at the rates indicated would be worth 45 years later.

Years in the future					
ROR*	30	40	"45"	50	x 2.25
2	$1,811	$2,208	$2,450	$2,692	$5,513
4	$3,243	$4,801	$5,954	$7,107	$13,397
6	$5,743	$10,286	$14,353	$18,420	$32,294
8	$10,063	$21,725	$34,313	$46,901	$77,204

*ROR = Rate of Return

So a little over 45 years later, had I invested the $2,250 I "saved" buying the car I could afford instead of the one I really wanted, that "savings," would be worth around:

- $5,513 if it earned 2%
- $13,397 if it earned 4%
- $32,294 if it earned 6%
- $77,204 if it earned 8%

Now imagine if by "living in poverty" for just ONE year when you could *afford* to spend more enabled you to save $10,000 to invest for your future. Use Table FVS-1 in Appendix A to calculate what that $10,000 could be worth 20, 30, or 40 years later.

A 1983 Mustang convertible gave me another "financial lesson." In 1983, Ford came out with a new Mustang convertible that looked a lot like the old ones. By then I COULD qualify for a loan, so I borrowed around $13,000 to buy a NEW Mustang convertible.

Thirty years later I still remember payments were around $318 / month. It's also the last time I bought a NEW car, because by the time I was ready to replace it, I had learned to calculate what the savings of buying a used car could mean to my future income.

CREATE A MILLIONAIRE BUDDY SYSTEM

One of the obstacles to accumulating wealth can be the people you spend time with.

If your friends have no interest in building wealth while you do, you may need to find new friends – *or at least spend more time with friends with common long term financial goals.*

Consider finding someone who also wants to accumulate wealth, and create a buddy system to help each other. You may find a new group of people who will be just as good friends, but will ***help*** you achieve your goals rather than be ***obstacles*** to your success.

Creating Future Spending

According to the Employee Benefit Research Institute (EBRI) 2016 Retirement Confidence survey, which surveys people who are working and have income, just 21% of those surveyed are very confident they can retire comfortably.

Included in their comments were ideas for workers to boost their savings and to think of current SAVINGS as future SPENDING. In other words, money saved today is really money that could be available for spending in the future.

I've found many people have difficulty visualizing what an investment today could be worth in future "spending," but they seem to "get it" when its explained as follows:

Suppose you are 31, expect to work until 60, start drawing from your investments at 61, and expect to live to 90.

The "Creating Future Spending" table assumes from 31 to 60 you invest $1,000 a year, then at 61 you start withdrawing the accumulated value of the $1,000 you had invested 30 years earlier.

The future value is shown based on assumed investment rates of 1% a year, 3% a year, 5% a year, and 7% a year so you can see how the rate of return your investments earn can impact the future amount of funds available to spend.

The table shows the future value of each individual $1,000 investment – 30 years later – assuming earnings were reinvested and earned the same annual rate of return.

For example, if each year for 30 years, you opened a separate investment account, invested $1,000 in that account, and through the following 30 years, each of those accounts earned 5% a year on the original investment and any earnings, each of those $1,000 investments, 30 years later, would be worth $4,322.

CREATING FUTURE SPENDING

				Value assuming a rate of return of			
Age	Invested		Age	1%	3%	5%	7%
31	$1,000		61	$1,348	$2,427	$4,322	$7,612
.....							
35	$1,000		65	$1,348	$2,427	$4,322	$7,612
....							
40	$1,000		70	$1,348	$2,427	$4,322	$7,612
.....			....				
45	$1,000		75	$1,348	$2,427	$4,322	$7,612
.....			.....				
50	$1,000		80	$1,348	$2,427	$4,322	$7,612
.....			.....				
55	$1,000		85	$1,348	$2,427	$4,322	$7,612
56	$1,000		86	$1,348	$2,427	$4,322	$7,612
57	$1,000		87	$1,348	$2,427	$4,322	$7,612
58	$1,000		88	$1,348	$2,427	$4,322	$7,612
59	$1,000		89	$1,348	$2,427	$4,322	$7,612
60	$1,000		90	$1,348	$2,427	$4,322	$7,612

Something to think about:

- A job creates "one time" income.
- Investments can create "recurring" income.

Investing a portion of each paycheck can help turn "one time" income into "recurring" income.

Book Review

RICH HABITS: The Daily Success Habits of Wealthy Individuals

by Thomas C. Corley

Rich Habits is less than 100 pages – but full of great information for those who want to accumulate wealth.

Many of the ideas proposed by the author are ones I live by and have recommended to clients over the years, so you may find many similarities in his comments to mine throughout this book.

Mr. Corley said he wrote the book when he realized so many of the people he advised (he was an accountant) were doing well and he wasn't. He interviewed successful people, as well as those who weren't, and created a "Rich Habit Training Program" based on ideas that worked for him and others to help people "re-program" themselves for greater success.

The training program consisted of 10 habits. Below are what I considered key ideas from the book:

1. To be successful you need to understand your strengths, and weaknesses. The recommendation was to make a sheet with two columns: on the left list BAD daily habits. On the right list their "opposite." For example, if a bad habit is "I smoke," change it to "I will not smoke today." Then create a checklist of good habits and check off each day those you did.

2. Time is too valuable to be wasted on things that have no tangible (ie: IDENTIFIABLE) value.

3. Successful people spend time with like-minded people and cut ties with people whose actions or comments undermine their quest for success.

4. Successful people live a balanced life.

5. Successful people focus on the possible.

6. Successful people practice "Rich Thinking." They see problems and obstacles as opportunities.

7. Successful people have long term, DEFINED goals and regularly monitor their progress and make adjustments as needed.

As in any book, one reader may take away different ideas than another. I encourage you to read the book for yourself and see what you get out of it that I may not have done.

Brown Bag Some Lifetime Income

Years ago, I learned a friend had no savings at all. But she went out to lunch every day. Even back in the 1980s, she typically spent $5 per day, or $25 a week. I suggested going out for lunch two days a week, bringing lunch from home (*we called it brown-bagging*) the other three days of the week, and encouraging coworkers to join her.

About six months later she told me she had done it and now had $300 in savings, more than she had ever had in savings at one time. It made me feel great to know such a simple change in daily habits could have such a beneficial effect in someone's life.

Much of what we do is just habit or stuff friends want to do. A key to building wealth is to exchange habits that cost money but don't really help you achieve your longer term financial goals for habits that can be just as much fun, but get you closer to your goal. A brown bag lunch with friends could be a good start to a more comfortable and financially secure future, and as an added incentive you might consider the following:

1. Unless you walk to where you're going to eat, gas costs should be included in the cost of lunch.

2. If you have to wait to get served, you may have to rush through your meal, so it probably isn't very relaxing.

This doesn't apply if you use your lunch hour to run errands, but if you are going out just to get away from the office, the following might give you some food (*pun intended*) for thought:

1. Find a place you can gather and bring your own lunch.

2. Spend lunch talking about whatever you would talk about if you went to a restaurant, OR
   a. If there's an electrical outlet where you eat, get a book on CD from the library and listen during lunch. You might even consider with business / self-help ideas you can discuss together.
   b. Each subscribe to a different magazine and share ideas you learn with each other.
   c. Start an investment club and build wealth together.

If you had a brown bag party with friends a couple times a week and saved $15 a week doing that 50 weeks a year, you'd each have $750 a year to invest in YOUR future instead of the future of the restaurant owner. If you did this for three years, you could accumulate the wealth detailed in the "Brown Bag It" table.

BROWN BAG IT

Year	3 years brown-bagging	Invested at 7% a year	7% a year MTE*	10 years brown-bagging	Invested at 7% a year	7% a year MTE*
1	$750	$750	$53	$750	$750	$53
2	$750	$1,553	$109	$750	$1,553	$109
3	$750	$2,411	$169	$750	$2,411	$169
4		$2,580	$181	$750	$3,330	$233
5		$2,761	$193	$750	$4,313	$302
.....						
10		$3,872	$271	$750	$10,362	$725
.....						
15		$5,430	$380		$14,534	$1,017
.....						
20		$7,616	$533		$20,384	$1,427
.....						
25		$10,682	$748		$28,590	$2,001
.....						
30		$14,983	$1,049		$40,099	$2,807

*MTE = **M**oney **T**ree **E**ffect (see Chapter "What's an MTE?")

In other words, you are still spending time with friends, probably eating a healthier lunch, in a way that could be worth several hundred dollars a year of extra income in the future, and may help some friends do the same.

J. Paul Getty was a Billionaire

Years ago, I read a book with the title "How to be Rich." It got my attention because it was written by a pretty reliable source: billionaire J. Paul Getty.

I believe almost anyone who TRULY wants to become a millionaire, CAN. But doing so may require very difficult CHOICES about your career, lifestyle, even your friends.

A common reason I often hear for someone having no savings is they never had "enough" income to be able to save. Since many investment can be started with less than $5.00 a day, I suggest it's not a lack of income, but the cost of a CHOSEN lifestyle that is the obstacle to saving. And one's lifestyle CAN be changed.

According to the website, www.millionairecorner.com, only about 1 in 4 millionaires inherited their wealth. The rest accumulated it on their own.

In the "Brown Bag Some Lifetime Income" chapter I shared the story of a friend who built wealth by bringing her lunch to work.

Another story that sticks with me was of a young, single dad. He had four children and a modest income. When I called him about investing he said he was interested but not yet ready. I asked him to get a 2-liter plastic bottle and put $2.00 in it each day, explaining if he did it for 60 days (*when I would call him back*) he would have enough to invest $50 to start, AND REALIZE HE COULD AFFORD TO KEEP DOING IT. When I called back, he had tried, but used it for an emergency. He asked me to call again. I called him two months later. Same story. When I called him two months after that and got the same EXCUSE, I told him if he really wasn't interested, just tell me and I wouldn't waste his time or mine. He made an appointment to come in and set up his plan.

When I checked with him six months later, he told me several times he had been tempted to call and stop, but found the money he needed through cutting his spending. (SMART MAN!!)

About 10 years later, I received a call he was in the hospital with cancer. Sadly, he passed away shortly after, HOWEVER ... his investment by then was worth $10,000, leaving each of his children $2,500 as a final legacy.

Sadly, many people who have less than $10,000 by age 50 had greater income and fewer expenses than this young man, but they never took some simple steps to do what he did.

The fact is someone earning $20,000 to start and receiving a 2% raise each year is likely to earn more than a million dollars in a typical 40 to 45-year career. The "Millionaire in a Lifetime" table illustrates this idea.

Moreover, if 10% of earnings each year were just saved (*earning nothing*) total savings would have been $125,220 at age 60 and $148,661 at age 65. Further, if those savings were invested and earned 7% a year, by 50 our million dollar earner would have been able to withdraw almost $6,000 a year for the rest of his/her life, and by age 65 more than $10,000 a year for the rest of his/her life.

Referencing the "Millionaire in a Lifetime" table that follows:

1. The second column (*earnings per year*) assumes income at 20 of $20,000, increasing by 2% each year.
2. The third column (*cumulative earnings*) is the total amount of income earned through the age indicated (*for example, by the end of age 25, total earnings would have added up to $126,162*).
3. The fourth column (*save 10% a year*) assumes 10% of each year's earnings is set aside, so the amount shown is just 10% of THAT YEAR's earnings.
4. The fifth column (*non-invested cumulative earnings*) assumes any money saved is not invested, but merely set aside and earning nothing through all those years.
5. The last column (*7% MTE*) illustrates the income that could be generated each year forward assuming the savings earned 7% a year and was withdrawn (spent) instead of invested.

MILLIONAIRE IN A LIFETIME

Age	Earnings per year (45 years)	Cumulative earnings	Save 10% a year	Non-invested cumulative savings	7% MTE*
20	$20,000	$20,000	$2,000	$2,000	$140
21	$20,400	$40,400	$2,040	$4,040	$283
22	$20,808	$61,208	$2,081	$6,121	$428
23	$21,224	$82,432	$2,122	$8,243	$577
24	$21,649	$104,081	$2,165	$10,408	$729
25	$22,082	$126,162	$2,208	$12,616	$883
.....					
30	$24,380	$243,374	$2,438	$24,337	$1,704
.....					
35	$26,917	$372,786	$2,692	$37,279	$2,609
.....					
40	$29,719	$515,666	$2,972	$51,567	$3,610
.....					
45	$32,812	$673,418	$3,281	$67,342	$4,714
.....					
50	$36,227	$847,589	$3,623	$84,759	$5,933
.....					
55	$39,998	$1,039,887	$4,000	$103,989	$7,279
.....					
60	***$44,161***	***$1,252,200***	***$4,416***	***$125,220***	***$8,765***
61	$45,044	$1,297,244	$4,504	$129,724	$9,081
62	$45,945	$1,343,189	$4,594	$134,319	$9,402
63	$46,864	$1,390,053	$4,686	$139,005	$9,730
64	$47,801	$1,437,854	$4,780	$143,785	$10,065
65	***$48,757***	***$1,486,611***	***$4,876***	***$148,661***	***$10,406***

*MTE = **M**oney **T**ree **E**ffect (see Chapter "What's an MTE?")

High income makes it easier, but priorities are the real key.

It's not the high cost of living, but the cost of living high that is the greater obstacle to wealth.

Can Borrowing Money Make You Richer

Some financial books talk about "good" debt and "bad" debt. I'd like to suggest you think of debt in terms of "profitable" and "unprofitable" debt.

Back in the early 1980s I had clients in their 50's who expected to work another 10 – 15 years, had little saved for retirement, but had equity in their homes.

Back then even 1-2 year CD's were paying 12%. (if only we had known to buy 10 year CD's or 30 year treasuries and lock in 14% or more) and a 15 year home mortgage averaged 16%. It might have seemed odd to recommend clients borrow money at 16% to invest it at 12%, but here was my reasoning.

1. For each $10,000 borrowed at 16% the monthly payment was around $147 or around $1800 a year.
2. The clients I recommended this to were likely to be working another 10-15 years and had sufficient income to make payments on the amount they would borrow.
3. Invested at 12%, the money borrowed would double every six years ("rule of 72"), so in six years the borrowed / invested $10,000 would be worth $20,000, and in another six years it would be worth $40,000. Moreover, by year 15 when the mortgage was paid off, if the investment continued to earn 12% a year, the originally borrowed $10,000 would have grown to over $54,000.
4. Even if CD rates dropped to 6% by then, $54,000 earning 6% a year would generate $3,240 a year, "forever." Money that could now be used to increase their retirement income in exchange for putting some of their home's equity to work while they could afford to make the payments.

What most people didn't think about is that the interest they were PAYING was on a declining balance because each payment partly reduced the amount of debt the interest was calculated on, while the interest they were EARNING on the investments was calculated on an increasing amount (compounding – i.e.: interest being earned on interest that had been reinvested).

The key to this idea is that each payment made reduced part of the principal, so the interest was paid on a declining balance, while the interest earned on the money invested was earned on an increasing balance.

The "Borrowed Wealth" table below shows this idea year by year.

BORROWED WEALTH, PART 1

$10,000 borrowed at 16%					$10,000 invested at 12%
Year	Payment	Interest owed	Principal reduction	Balance owed	End of year value
1	$1,800	$1,600	$200	$9,800	$11,200
2	$1,800	$1,568	$232	$9,568	$12,544
3	$1,800	$1,531	$269	$9,299	$14,049
4	$1,800	$1,488	$312	$8,987	$15,735
5	$1,800	$1,438	$362	$8,625	$17,623
6	$1,800	$1,380	$420	$8,205	$19,738
7	$1,800	$1,313	$487	$7,717	$22,107
8	$1,800	$1,235	$565	$7,152	$24,760
9	$1,800	$1,144	$656	$6,496	$27,731
10	$1,800	$1,039	$761	$5,736	$31,058
11	$1,800	$918	$882	$4,853	$34,785
12	$1,800	$777	$1,023	$3,830	$38,960
13	$1,800	$613	$1,187	$2,643	$43,635
14	$1,800	$423	$1,377	$1,266	$48,871
15	$1,800	$202	$1,598	–$332	$54,736

Rates on both mortgages and investments are lower as this is being written (2016). The rate on a 15 year mortgage is averaging less than

3.5% while a diversified* investment portfolio over the same 15 years might "reasonably" be assumed to earn 5%**.

If you borrowed money at 4% a year, the annual payments per $1,000 on a 15 year loan would be around $85.80, a total of $1,290 over 15 years. ($290 of interest, $1,000 repayment of borrowed funds), while $1,000 invested at 5% over 15 years would be worth $2,079, for a profit of $1,079. (See table: Borrowed Wealth, Part 2).

Which means for each $1,000 borrowed using these assumptions, you effectively turned $290 of interest into $1,079 of new wealth. Money YOU didn't have to work to create. The money you borrowed created it for you.

BORROWED WEALTH, PART 2

$1,000 borrowed at 4%					$1,000 invested at 5%
Year	Payment	Interest owed	Principal reduction	Balance owed	End of year value
1	$58	$40	$18	$982	$1,050
2	$58	$39	$19	$963	$1,103
3	$58	$39	$19	$944	$1,158
4	$58	$38	$20	$924	$1,216
5	$58	$37	$21	$903	$1,276
.....					
10	$58	$32	$26	$784	$1,629
.....					
20	$58	$20	$38	$464	$2,653
.....					
25	$58	$12	$46	$250	$3,386
26	$58	$10	$48	$202	$3,556
27	$58	$8	$50	$152	$3,733
28	$58	$6	$52	$101	$3,920
29	$58	$4	$54	$47	$4,116
30	$58	$2	$56	–$10	$4,322

Note: Due to rounding $57.29 to $58 for calculations, the actual total investment shown in the above table adds up to $1,740, not $1,719.

*DIVERSIFIED: diversification does not guarantee a profit or protect against a loss in a declining market. It is a method used to help manage investment risk.

**Figures quoted are for illustrative purposes only and are not necessarily indicative of past or future results on any specific investment. They do not include consideration of the time value of money, taxes, inflation, or fluctuation in principal. Your investments may grow at higher or lower rates.

UNINVESTED MONEY IS LIKE SERVANTS STANDING BY NOT BEING TOLD WHAT TO DO.

Do You Have a Mission Statement?

About 25 years ago, mission statements, vision statements, and "visioning" became a focus of many organizations, both corporate and government.

As best as I have been able to tell, the goal of either the mission or vision statement was to create an easy to remember statement to help employees of the organization be able to evaluate whether what they were doing would help their employer accomplish its mission, and for customers, a way of better understanding what an organization was trying to accomplish with their product or service.

In my personal opinion one of the best mission statements I've seen with respect to making it easy for employees to know the goal of the company and evaluate whether what they were doing helped the company accomplish that mission, and that made the founders of the business very wealthy at a young age is the following:

"A COMPUTER ON EVERY DESK AND IN EVERY HOME."

Imagine you worked at a company where there were constant reminders that the goal of your employer was to reach a point that every desk, in every home, had a computer.

Would it be easy for you to know if what you were doing each day was helping the company reach that goal?

If you aren't familiar with that particular mission statement, it's the mission statement of a company called *Microsoft*.

While even today there may not be "a computer on every desk in every home," hundreds of millions of computers using *Microsoft* software have been sold, are still in operation, and Bill Gates – in spite of giving billions to charities and his own foundation - is (at least as of 2015) the richest man in the world.

Talk about the power of a clear and concise "mission statement"!

Which brings me to YOU. Do you truly want to be wealthy? Are you willing to do what it takes (as long as it's legal and ethical) to reach your personal financial goal?

Then consider taking this initial challenge to create your own "Personal Wealth Mission Statement."

PERSONAL WEALTH MISSION STATEMENT.

I will have $ ________________ on or before ____________ (Date) at which time I plan to work only if and when I choose.

I am going to save and invest $___________ this year, and increase the amount I save/invest each year by _____%.

I am willing to make the following three changes in my current spending to make that goal a reality:

1. ______________________________________
2. ______________________________________
3. ______________________________________

As ever, the CHOICE, is yours. But imagine if each time you went to invest or spend, time or money, you asked yourself whether that use of your time or money was likely to help you reach YOUR personal goal.

Invest Yourself Out of a Job

While there are many who regularly walk a mile a day (including my 93-year-old mother) the thought of running 26 miles is mind-boggling to many (including me). Even thinking of WALKING 26 miles would cause many to say "no way."

Marathoners tell me the secret is to focus on getting from one mile marker to the next. Assuming the ultimate purpose of investing is to be able to live off your "money," a similar approach can be used to build wealth by focusing on replacing wages one <u>*hour*</u> at a time.

The basic concept is simple: to replace what you earn by working with income from investments, one hour at a time. The underlying formula for this is "I / R = P" where

- "I" stands for the hourly earned income to be "replaced" with investment income.

- "R" stands for the percent rate of return your investments are assumed to earn per year.

- "P" stands for the principal (amount) you would need to invest at rate "R" to generate one hour of income per year.

Start with your gross hourly income. Since investment income is not subject to FICA taxes, to "replace" one hour a day of income from work with investment income, you need enough investment INCOME to generate your "net of FICA" hourly earnings.

For example, assume your net income is $10 an hour. If you invested $200 and it earned 5% a year, it would generate the same $10 you earned working an hour.

INCOME (PER HOUR) / INTEREST (RATE EARNED) = PRINCIPAL (INVESTMENT) NEEDED
\$10.00 / .05 = \$200.00

The idea with this "wage replacement" concept is to "buy your freedom" one hour, then one day, then one week, and so on until you have enough investments to generate, year after year, income equal to what you earn working for a full year.

If we continue to assume your earned income is \$10.00 an hour.

1. To replace an 8-hour day of wages, every year, "forever," you would need investments of \$1,600 (\$200 x 8).

2. To replace a 40-hour week of wages, every year, "forever," you would need investments of \$8,000 (\$200 x 40).

3. To replace the income, you would have earned working 40 hours a week for 52 weeks, every year, "forever," you would need investments of \$416,000 (\$8,000 x 52).

Like 26 miles, \$416,000 may seem a long way off, but if you focus on replacing "one hour at a time" of wages, you may find it's not as far off as you expected.

VERY IMPORTANT NOTE: This example is to show you the "thought process" in calculating the amount needed to generate on an ongoing income equivalent to \$10 / hour. And most importantly, the amount calculated assumes the same amount of income each year, with no increase allowed for increases in the cost of living.

A good investment is like an employer you don't have to work for to get paid.

Instead of YOU getting up to earn income, your INVESTMENTS do it for you.

Know the Details

Assumptions are great, except when they are wrong.

Many investments have both initial sales charges and annual fees. To help clients relate, I often use a new car/used car analogy assuming the new car will cost more but the used car has higher annual expenses.

Suppose a new car cost $30,000, a good used one costs $23,000, and you plan to keep either for seven years. For simplicity assume they have equal future trade-in value. If the maintenance cost for the used car is $1,000 a year higher, the comparative cost of ownership for each would be $30,000. If the higher maintenance of the used car was only $500 a year higher, seven year costs would be $3,500 and ownership of the used car would be less. If maintenance costs for the used car were $1,200 a year higher, the new car would have lower "cost of ownership."

Now, suppose investment A costs $3,000 up front, and investment B costs $500 a year more to "own."

(Excluding the effects of the time value of money.) If you plan to keep the investment more than six years, the cost of ownership would be less to pay the up-front fee of $3,000.

As you invest, be sure to understand all the cost involved in owning an investment.

SUCCESS = achieving your DESIRED outcome.

Love Those "Free" Massages

This assumes the only actual purpose / value of having "money" is what you can use it for. So let me offer a perspective I've used and might be useful for you as well.

I can easily afford to buy a new car. I can also afford to get a massage a week without damaging my lifetime financial security.

But getting "something for nothing," as long as it is legal and ethical, seems to be part of my DNA.

Even as a child I loved getting my back scratched. I came up with a plan that may seem silly, but it worked. My sister was around 3 at the time. She liked to draw. So I would let her draw on my back with her nails, as long as she "scratched out" each picture before she could draw another one.

I still love to have my back scratched, but I also LOVE getting a massage. It is one of my true pleasures.

Several years ago I discovered the local "Academy of Cosmetology." Massages are by students in the massage program. I've never had a bad massage there, and even better, they only cost $25.00, plus tip. But I like it even more when I can get a great massage for "free."

Here's how I figured I got several years of "free" massages.

When my Honda Prelude started costing more in monthly repairs than payments would be on a replacement, I went looking for a replacement car.

If I bought a new Honda, it would have cost around $20,000. Instead, I found a lightly used Honda, this time an Accord, that cost $12,000. It worked just as well as a new car would have done to get me from where I was to where I needed to go, but not even counting higher taxes and insurance on the new car, that's an immediate saving of $8,000.

Since this was basically "found money," my plan was to use what I saved as my "massage fund." I figured if I got a massage twice a month, and spent $50 per massage, my total cost would be $1,200 a year. Assuming the money earned 7% a year, the "Free Massages" table below shows how I figured my "car" would pay for seven or eight years of massages:

FREE MASSAGES

Year	Car savings invested	Cost of massages	End of Year balance
1	$8,000	$1,200	$7,276
2		$1,200	$6,501
3		$1,200	$5,672
4		$1,200	$4,785
5		$1,200	$3,836
6		$1,200	$2,821
7		$1,200	$1,734
8		$1,200	$572

Moreover, I drove that car for 10 years, again bought a used car and "psychologically," I figure I have another six or so years of "free" massages, even though the cost of a massage is now a little higher.

Massages may not be something you enjoy, but my guess is there are other things you enjoy that cost money and would be fun to pay for with money you saved by buying a less expensive car than you could afford.

It's all a matter of CHOICE.

The Magic Pocket

There are a variety of definitions of wealth, but most seem to focus on "an abundance of valuable possessions or money."

But what is considered "an abundance of money" to one person may seem like poverty to another. Not that long ago, if you had a million dollars, you were probably considered wealthy, and even today, less than one out of ten American households have a million or more in assets that could produce or be converted to producing spendable income. For many, wealth is tied up in "possessions" that actually become liabilities if their sources of income (*needed to pay to keep those possessions insured and maintained*) suddenly cease or decline.

For an example of that you need look no further than someone who purchased a home, but with a mortgage. If they lose the source of income used to pay the mortgage, unless the home can be sold for more than the amount of the remaining mortgage, that house is really not an asset, but a "possession," and a potential liability.

While there is no single definition of "wealth" I offer this for your consideration:

> ***Wealth provides its owner (or the person who controls it) with the ability / means to generate income without needing to have a "customer" to provide a "paycheck."***

In other words, having other financial resources that could be used if a current source of income ceases.

Since the idea of being free to do what you want means, for most people, being able to work only by choice, if at all, then this definition of wealth means being able to convert what you own into money that can pay for the lifestyle you desire to live.

Recently a client sent me what was actually a joke, but it had an incredible message I wanted to share:

As the story went, each time this man ordered a meal at this restaurant, when the bill came, he reached into his pocket and always had the exact amount to give the waitress.

Day after day he ordered the same thing, until one day he came in with a friend, and again, when the bill was presented, he pulled the exact amount needed out of his pocket.

When the waitress finally asks how he can always have the exact amount of the bill in his pocket, he tells her he found a bottle, rubbed it, and a genie appeared. When asked what he wished, he said "if I ever had to pay for anything, I would just put my hand in my pocket and the right amount of money would always be there."

As the waitress noted, he would always be rich, regardless of whether his investments earned a particular rate of return, regardless of how long he lived, and regardless of how much the cost of living increased.

While it is unlikely any of us are going to find a bottle with a genie that will grant us a similar wish, one way to be able to buy whatever you might want or need in the future is to create as complete and realistic a spending plan as you can based on your desired lifestyle, other sources of income you are likely to receive, expected increases in YOUR cost of living, YOUR life expectancy, YOUR investment risk tolerance, and the tax environment you are likely to experience during the years you would like work to be an OPTION.

Meet Me Half Way

Thirty years ago or so, I was meeting with a young couple who wanted to get started building wealth for their future. They had a nice home, both were working, but they hadn't been saving.

As we talked, it came out that each week the husband put $50 in his wallet for his weekly spending. My suggestion was that he cut that back to $25 a week and see how it went, and that I would come back in a couple months to see how they did.

He said there was no way he could make it through the week, but was willing to try. When I called to set up the meeting a couple months later, they said they were ready to get started.

I met with them again to do the paperwork to start their IRA's, and asked how the $25 a week plan was working. As I expected, he said he found he had just as much left at the end of the week as he had when he started with $50.

Now imagine for 3 years he invested that $25 a week, except for 2 weeks of vacation when that $25 was spent. $25 a week saved times 50 weeks per year = $1,250.00 per year. The "Meet Me Half Way" chart shows the potential of this small CHOICE:

MEET ME HALF WAY

Year	Saved	Invested at 7%	7% MTE*
1	$1,250	$1,250	$88
2	$1,250	$2,588	$181
3	$1,250	$4,019	$281
4		$4,300	$301
5		$4,601	$322
.....			
10		$6,453	$452
.....			
15		$9,051	$634
.....			
20		$12,694	$889

*MTE = **M**oney **T**ree **E**ffect (see Chapter "What's an MTE?")

Whether he stopped reinvesting at 10 years, or 20, that's not a bad lifetime income supplement in exchange for meeting his future half way for just three years!!!

HERE'S A CHALLENGE FOR YOU: make a list of everything you can remember buying (or paying in bills) in the past month and see if it adds up to your take-home pay. If the income and expenses don't match, consider getting a 3"x5" spiral notebook and for one month, write down every single penny you spend. At the end of the month, see if you can account for all your income, then go compare it to what you wrote down in the notebook.

A key to successful wealth accumulation is to understand what a dollar not spent today could be worth in the future.

You Can't Change the Past

But you CAN "create" your future

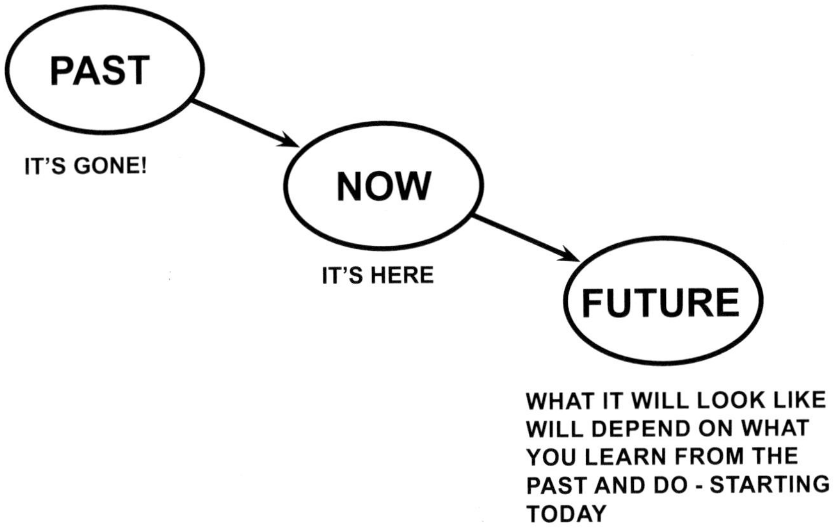

Life is a period of challenges and CHOICES, obstacles and opportunities, lessons to be learned and mistakes to be made.

Past CHOICES can't be changed. But you CAN learn from them, and make new CHOICES that could put you onto your desired course.

For example, even if you didn't start saving for retirement when you first started working, you can start now to find fun and creative ways to still enjoy life while spending less, and investing what you don't spend to work on "catching up."

Essentially what you are doing is substituting the funds that investing earlier might have earned by "doing things differently" moving forward.

One of my favorite quotes is the Serenity Prayer, by Reinhold Niebuhr (Wikipedia) first used in 1934.

***"God grant me the serenity to accept the things I cannot change,
the courage to change the things I can,
and the wisdom to know the difference."***

But I love a fourth line I saw attributed to General Omar Bradley that I think offers a really important philosophy to consider:

"But God grant me the courage not to give up no matter how difficult it may seem."

After all, wealth rarely just lands in your pocket. According to a survey on *www.millionairecorner.com,* the top three factors for obtaining wealth weren't magic. They were factors available to just about anyone: Hard work, Education, and Smart investing.

If you feel some of the decisions / choices you made in the past were not necessarily the best (i.e.: "mistakes"), you might consider a thought from one of my favorite authors, Richard Bach, that mistakes – at least the first time they are made - are just unexpected opportunities to learn something new (*and hopefully not repeat that same mistake again*). And please consider sharing what you learn to save others from the same potential cost / pain.

Moving forward, as you are confronted with CHOICES to make, take a minute to think, just a little, about how the CHOICE you make will affect your future.

Key to investing:

Buying the funding needed to finance a desired lifestyle, not just investments.

The Mathematics of Finance

I love math. Maybe because it always came easily to me, and I liked that when a problem was solved correctly, you got the same answer each time you used the same data. But I also know most people generally want to have as little to do with it as possible.

The problem for those who don't want to deal with math is that math is the underlying foundation of most personal finance calculations. Professors Annamaria Lusardi and Olivia S. Mitchell found an understanding of compound interest and the effects of inflation are linked to wealth accumulation. It's possible that learning some fundamental math concepts could enhance your own personal wealth potential.

Four basic values are generally factors in most "wealth" calculations:

1. The amount of time you have to achieve your goal.
2. The (average) rate of return you expect your investments will earn.
3. The amount of money to be invested – either as a single amount or annual investments.
4. For multiple year investments, the percent increase in the annual amount invested.

When these four factors are known, it's just a mathematical calculation to find the answer to most "wealth" calculations.

KEY POINT: If the value of one factor is increased, ***to reach the SAME goal***, the value of one or more of the other factors would decrease. Which also means that when there are limits on one or more of those factors, the desired goal may not be achievable.

Financial Independence is about having enough "money" to enjoy life without NEEDING to work.

The Power of Repetition

As I was reviewing the draft of this book, I realized the examples I've provided may seem to be almost identical to each other.

It's true. The general format is often the same. But what changes are the ideas. Not everyone is willing to live in a smaller home or drive used cars to accumulate wealth, so I've included dozens of ideas for saving money that I've used, or clients have used and shared with me. The reason these calculations are frequently repeated is that I believe the more you look at those numbers, the more you can "put yourself in that scenario," the greater the potential for you to really UNDERSTAND the potential for creating wealth from even small changes in spending.

Consider a quote attributed to Confucius over 2,000 years ago:

"Tell me, and I will forget.
Show me, and I may remember.
Involve me, and I will understand."

Personally, I find I have to write something down to truly remember it.

Think of the top athletes. You don't have to be a sports fan to be aware that many credit constant PRACTICE - repeating one golf stroke, or one basketball throw, or one soccer kick, OVER AND OVER until that action is second nature - as the foundation for their success.

If being able to visualize the potential future wealth from spending less today and investing it becomes second nature to you because you keep doing those calculations, it becomes much easier to see the potential cost, or benefit of even small CHOICES you make each day. And maybe you can become as talented at building wealth as the Michael Jordan, Tiger Woods, Wayne Gretzky, or Serena Williams are in their chosen field.

It can help to become adept at using the "RULE OF 72" – a simple shortcut you can easily do on paper, or even in your head, to estimate future living costs or future value of an investment. If you aren't familiar with this, you are not alone. Here is how it works:

- If you divide the interest rate you expect your investments to earn into 72, the answer is the number of years it will take for your investment to double. For example, if your investment earned 4% a year, it would double in 18 years (72 / 4 = 18).

- If you divide the inflation rate into 72, it tells you how many years it will take for the cost of living to double. For example, if you anticipate the cost of living will increase 3% / year, it will take 24 years for the cost of living to double (72 / 3 = 24 years).

TEST YOURSELF (answers below):

1. You expect your cost of living to increase 2% a year. How many years will it take for your cost of living to DOUBLE?
2. If you invest $1,000 and it earns 7% a year, how much would it be worth in 40 years?

Being able to do those calculations quickly and easily might make it easier to see the benefits of making small changes in your current spending for the potential to have more money to spend later on.

Answers:

1. 36 years
2. At 7% it doubles roughly every 10 years. That means in 10 years it would double to $2,000, in ANOTHER 10 year (20 total) it would double again to $4,000, in ANOTHER 10 years (total 30) it would double AGAIN, to $8,000, and in another 10 years (which brings you to year 40), it would double AGAIN, to $16,000.

The Quarter Inch Hole

For years, I've suggested to business owners as they market their product or service to assume a potential customer is asking "WIIFM?" - i.e.: "what's in it (your product) for me (the customer)."

A concept I read about years ago, noted while a customer may ask for a quarter inch drill, what they REALLY want is a quarter inch HOLE. They don't care if the hole is made by a drill, a hole punch, or a blowtorch. They just want to make a quarter inch HOLE.

In finance, you may ask for an IRA, mutual fund, or bond, but what you likely REALLY want is something that will provide income whether you continue to work or not.

Our attitudes toward money are often formed early in life as we watch our parents actions and listen to their words. Those attitudes can be very difficult to break unless we honestly look at ourselves and decide - for ourselves - the role money will play in our lives.

Raise Some Fun Money

While no one is guaranteed a raise, consider the example of someone who starts working at 25 earning $25,000 a year, earns 3% more each year, and works to age 55 (30 years). Assume HALF of each year's raise is spent, but the other half is invested earning 7%, and at some point in time, earnings from those investments were spent each year instead of invested.

By year 10, $5,003 would have been accumulated, enough to withdraw $350 a year to spend, each and every year after, without using the accumulated $5,003.

RAISE SOME FUN MONEY, PART 1

Year	Income	Raise	50% of raise	Invested at 7%	7% MTE*
1	$25,000				
2	$25,750	$750	$375	$375	$26
3	$26,523	$773	$386	$788	$55
4	$27,318	$796	$398	$1,240	$87
5	$28,138	$820	$410	$1,737	$122
.....					
10	$32,619	$950	$475	$5,003	$350
......					
20	$43,838	$1,277	$638	$17,466	$1,223
.....					
30	$58,914	$1,716	$858	$44,603	$3,122

ROR = Rate of return,
*MTE = **M**oney **T**ree **E**ffect (see Chapter "What's an MTE?")

And if this same person worked to 65, for a total of 40 years.

RAISE SOME FUN MONEY, PART 2

Year	Income	Raise	50% of raise	Invested at 7%	7% MTE*
31	$60,682	$1,767	$884	$48,609	$3,403
32	$62,502	$1,820	$910	$52,922	$3,705
33	$64,377	$1,875	$938	$57,564	$4,029
34	$66,308	$1,931	$966	$62,559	$4,379
35	$68,298	$1,989	$995	$67,933	$4,755
36	$70,347	$2,049	$1,024	$73,713	$5,160
37	$72,457	$2,110	$1,055	$79,928	$5,595
38	$74,631	$2,174	$1,087	$86,610	$6,063
39	$76,870	$2,239	$1,119	$93,792	$6,565
40	$79,176	$2,306	$1,153	$101,511	$7,106

ROR = Rate of return
*MTE = **M**oney **T**ree **E**ffect (see Chapter "What's an MTE?")

Which means if a 25 year old invested (at 7% a year) half their assumed raises each year, by age 65, they would have $101,511, enough at the assumed 7% ROR to withdraw $7,106 each and every year after, while still spending half their annual raise through the years.

Would You Trade $2,000 for $1,000?

Probably not if we were talking about doing it today.

But what if by cutting your spending by $2,000 for just **ONE** year, and leaving it invested for 30 years, starting in year 30 you would be able to withdraw almost $1,000, each and every year, basically "forever"?

TRADING $2,000 for $1,000

Year	Invested	Value at 7% a year	7% MTE*
1	$2,000	$2,000	$140
2		$2,140	$150
3		$2,290	$160
4		$2,450	$172
5		$2,622	$184
6		$2,805	$196
7		$3,001	$210
8		$3,212	$225
9		$3,436	$241
10		$3,677	$257
...	...	...	
15		$5,157	$361
...	...	...	
20		$7,233	$506
...	...	...	
25		$10,145	$710
...	...	...	
30		$14,229	$996

*MTE = **M**oney **T**ree **E**ffect (see Chapter "What's an MTE?")

So assuming your $2,000 earned 7% a year, by reducing your spending less than $6.00 a day for just ***ONE*** year, with TIME as your partner in wealth, you would be able to withdraw $996, each year, for as long as you live. And have over $14,000 left at the end.

It's your CHOICE.

From $12,000 to $150,000 in 157,680,000 (Or So) Seconds

In November 1997, a "money makeover" story was published in the Orlando Sentinel. It told of a couple who in 1992, five years earlier, were in their 30's and had acquired all the trappings of middle class success - home, cars, health club, evenings out at nice restaurants, etc.

They were also $12,000 in debt - NOT COUNTING THEIR MORTGAGE!

When the article was written, they still had a home and transportation. They still did things for entertainment - including three trips to Europe in the previous five years. BUT ... THEY ALSO HAD NO DEBT AND A NEST EGG OF $150,000 IN INVESTMENTS.

How did they do that?

Instead of spending $5,000 a month, as they had been doing five years earlier, they made the decision to live on $2,000 a month and invest the rest.

You may not want to simplify your life as much as they did, but it doesn't mean you can't go from debt to a decent beginning toward "BEING RICH" just by making some minor, and not so minor, adjustments in HOW YOU MANAGE your time and activities.

This might give you some incentive: The 7% MTE (***M**oney **T**ree **E**ffect*) on their $150,000 is $10,500. That means if they just left the $150,000 invested and it earned 7% a year, each and every year they would be able to withdraw $10,500 to spend on what THEY want, for the rest of their life, all in exchange for five years of living well below their means.

Wondering about the 157 million seconds in the chapter title?

- It took this couple 5 years to go from -$12,000 to +$150,000.
- 5 years times 365 days / year = 1,825 days.
- 1,825 days times 24 hours / day = 43,800 hours.
- 43,800 hours times 3,600 seconds / hour - 157,680,000 seconds in 5 years (*excluding leap years*).

You may not be able to find $3,000 a month to save, but I'll bet you could find $50 a week (or find a way to earn an extra $50 a week) to convert from current spending to a source of future wealth if you really tried.

When you know where you are going, it's more likely you will get there.

A Very Expensive Drink

Our local sheriff has a great sense of humor. Outside an office at the local mall is a car he had painted with a unique message on the side and back windows shown in the pictures below.

On the driver's side (first picture) it says "ride in the front seat \$24" and "ride in the back seat \$8,000" The back window (second picture) lists the cost of getting caught DUI (\$8,000).

So let's take just a single time of driving under the influence and getting caught, versus having a designated driver, or calling a "we drive/you ride" service, and investing the \$8,000 it would have cost you in an investment earning an average 7% a year.

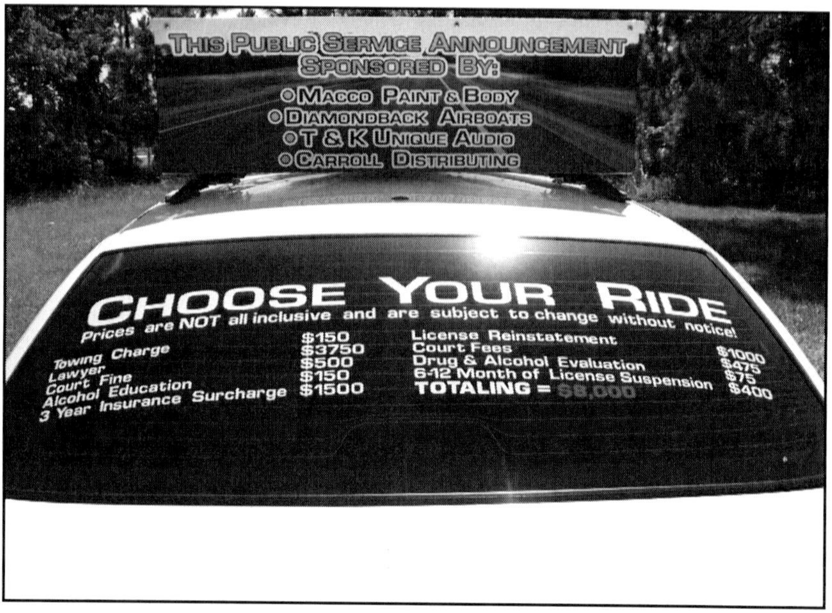

Using Table FVS-1 in Appendix A, try calculating the future value of that $8,000 if you reinvested the earnings for 10, 20, or 30 years. The results should be:

- $15,736 in 10 years (7% MTE = $1,102 per year)
- $30,960 in 20 years (7% MTE = $2,167 per year)
- $60,896 in 30 years (7% MTE = $4,263 per year)

To calculate the 7% "**M**oney **T**ree **E**ffect (MTE)," you would multiply each of those amounts by .07. (Results shown above in parentheses).

Something to think about next time you go out partying with friends and consider driving home when you've been drinking.

A Millionaire Perspective

Not everyone has the temperament or personality to be a business owner, but most people have the potential to create a "Wealth Pantry." (See picture in "Nothing is Guaranteed.")

Business owners generally think in terms of Revenue, expenses and PROFIT, but employees rarely consider the difference between what they earn and what they spend as personal "profit."

In "The Millionaire Mind," the millionaires Dr. Stanley interviewed shared what I found an interesting perspective: SAVINGS as PROFITS and INVESTMENTS as "INVENTORY."

This caught my attention because when I think of "inventory," I can visualize an "item" sitting on a shelf, waiting to be used or sold, and it made me visualize my investment portfolio as "shares of companies" (or funds), sitting on a shelf waiting to be used, not just as a nebulous "asset" with a value on a piece of paper.

As a thought, if you own stock in a specific company, visualize what the company makes sitting in a storeroom waiting to be sold to create income for you.

While this may sound silly, being able to "see" the underlying source of income for the investments you own can help to better understand how those investments can be a source of wealth, and income, for your future.

A WEALTH CHOICES CHECK LIST FOR YOU

Yes---No

_____ _____ I know when I would like to retire (years from now).

_____ _____ I know how long I am likely to live.

_____ _____ I have estimated the annual cost of being retired.

_____ _____ I have a three-six-month emergency fund.

_____ _____ I have estimated the annual increase in spending I will need to finance my desired future lifestyle.

_____ _____ I understand past performance of various investments cannot be guaranteed, and am familiar with historical investment returns.

_____ _____ I understand investments have commissions and fees that can reduce my investment return.

_____ _____ I BELIEVE IN MY ABILITY TO ACHIEVE MY GOALS AND (if needed) AM WILLING TO CHANGE MY CURRENT LIFESTYLE TO ACHIEVE MY DESIRED FUTURE.

> ***"Ignoring reality will not make it go away or change it, but doing so will often leave you to suffer the consequences of that CHOICE." - Ilene Davis***

Book Review

MIDDLE CLASS MILLIONAIRE

by Russ Allen Prince and Lewis Schiff

Following are some of the observations or conclusions the authors made about what they call Middle Class Millionaires (MCM) – people who have a net worth of $1 million to $10 million who created their wealth instead of inheriting it, and who have a mindset different than those who start in similar financial circumstances but stay "middle net worth" (MNW).

A key part of their attitude may be what each considers the amount of net worth needed to be "wealthy." For those who are not of the MCM mindset, $2.3 million is considered sufficient. For MCM's, it is $24 million.

MCMs are more likely to focus on drawing financial gain from their work and were less inclined to be discouraged by failure. A key part in choosing a career is its prospective financial rewards. Only 2% of MCM's believe in "love what you do and the money will follow."

MCMs are achievement oriented and assume most problems could be solved with the right people and creative thinking. To them, work represents opportunity. They are willing to work hard to achieve their financial goals and believe their own prosperity can be enhanced when they partner with people who have common interests.

MCMs are willing to pay someone else to do tasks that are not related to their unique abilities. They will LEVERAGE the talent of others. The goal of a typical MCM is to get ahead while most who remain middle class just want to keep up. They will choose a career more on the basis of its PROSPECTIVE financial rewards, not necessarily the immediate ones.

They are willing to take lower pay at a startup company in exchange for equity in the company that might be worth much more later.

MCMs are three times more likely to belong to formal, or even informal, networking groups. Networking is a key part of their life. They see networking as a way to connect with people they can turn to for information. That networking isn't about "selling," but about building relationships that may have future value – for both parties when possible.

KEY POINT: THE RICH WORK FOR THE POOR. The rich make their money by getting lots of poor people to pay them for a product or service. MCMs believe creating value for other people is the path to riches for themselves. For example, when they have a need, and there isn't a company to fulfill that need, their solution is to start such a company.

Can You Drive a Stick Shift?

I know, a strange question in a book on building wealth, but in trying to explain my concept for this book to a friend, I commented the hardest part was the minute math is mentioned, many people just say they don't want to deal with it. But if you can't figure out how much you need to invest, and at what rate, to get from where you are financially to where you want to be, it can be far more difficult to make "wealthy" financial, and even life, CHOICES.

In the process of the conversation, I ended up commenting that it reminded me of when I was first learning to drive. While one car my parents had was automatic transmission, the other had a stick shift.

Having to figure out when to use the clutch, when to shift, and so on was not something I wanted to do. But in spite of my whining (*I was 15, what do you expect*) that it was hard, and I didn't want to damage the car by doing it wrong and other such excuses, my dad insisted I learn to drive a stick shift, explaining a time might come when the only car available was a stick shift (*NOTE: My dad was an Eagle Scout, so being prepared was part of his DNA.*).

Anyway, I did learn to drive that stick shift. And years later, sure enough, my car was in the shop, and the only car they had as a loaner had a manual transmission (stick shift).

Learning the math of finance is really pretty similar. Not something most people want to learn how to do, but something that could ultimately enable them to become the millionaire many have the potential to become.

Don't allow fear of the unknown to be an obstacle to achieving YOUR financial goals.

Crock-Pot Party

I ***LOVE*** my Crock-Pot! I bought my first one over 30 years ago, I used it to make soup (*particularly chicken soup when I got a cold*), the Swedish meatballs I make for parties, chili, stews, spaghetti sauce, corned beef and cabbage for St. Patty's day, and so much more.

There are dozens of great meals you can make with 10-15 minutes "preparation" where once you put all the ingredients in the pot, all you have to do is turn it on, set a timer if needed, go have fun or relax, and let the Crock-Pot do its magic.

I have six or seven Crock-Pots of different sizes, all bought on sale or at thrift stores, so my total cost for all of them is about $150.

If I had invested that $150 and it earned 7% a year, it would generate about $11 a year. I'm confident I've saved far more than that through the years, plus I've saved hundreds of hours of time, and had healthy food to eat.

I figure most of the dishes I make for parties, even counting having to cut up the ingredients, generally take less than 30 minutes to prepare.

At any rate, I consider the cost of my Crock-Pots an investment that has paid off handsomely year after year in both money saved on making things myself versus buying prepared, and in the time spent (*since I'm either listening to the news or a book on tape when I'm getting everything ready*).

Following are several Crock Pot ideas I've shared through the years:

<u>HEALTHIER EATING WHILE SAVING MONEY.</u>

I really enjoy soup. Although there were several cans of soup in the pantry, after learning at Metabolic Research Center about how much sodium and preservatives – bad for both health and weight - are in almost anything in cans, I didn't want to use them, so I went out, bought frozen chicken breasts and fresh and frozen veggies, cut up the veggies, and put them and a couple frozen chicken breasts in the Crock-Pot. Other than a couple bouillon cubes for added flavor and some non-salt seasoning and pepper, everything I used was healthy and natural. Result: 5 quarts of chicken soup for about $7.00. It took more time to ladle it into containers than it did to put the ingredients into a pot and let them cook overnight. And there was a lot more chicken and vegetables in my soup than in the canned version. What the Crock-Pot made while I was sleeping was equal to eight 20-oz cans. Even at $1.25 on sale, that would be $10.00. Maybe $3.00 in savings doesn't mean much to you, but if you had even that savings each week, it still adds up to over $150 a year.

SAVING TIME, MONEY AND STRESS

A couple (*I'll call them Bob and Sue*) that met with me was planning to get married in six months and wanted to be debt free by then.

We went through their budget and talked about ideas to save money over the next six months. I shared some ideas, including Bob loaning money (*for the half percent rate he was currently earning on his savings*) to Sue so she could pay her credit cards (*that had interest rates of 10% or more*), and use what she saved paying a lower interest rate for their honeymoon. We talked about how much they spent eating out, or at the cafeteria at work, and other ideas. About three months later, they asked to meet again. They had paid off the credit cards, but now wanted to save money for the honeymoon.

As we reviewed their updated spending plan, it showed about 15% of their joint income being spent on food, much still on eating out several times a week and buying lunch at work.

When I brought that up, they said they were just so busy at work, that by the time they got home, they were too tired and stressed out to make dinner. So, I reminded them of the Crock-Pot discussion.

Here's the funny part. They said they had actually done that, but with the holidays, they got busy with dinners with family and friends, going out for work parties and such, and forgot about it. But they also said when they had made Crock-Pot meals at home, they had been less stressed, ate better, and spent less.

Here's their story: They both work full-time. Her children stay with them on weekends and they often attend the kid's activities during the week. They figured because *"they didn't have time or were too tired to make dinner,"* they generally went out to dinner one or two days a week and spent $25-$50 each time.

I suggested if they thought about the time it took to get to the restaurant, wait if it was busy, eat, the drive back home, they probably spent an hour each time. They said more like two hours.

Anyway, they started laughing at themselves, so this is the plan we developed: since they generally went grocery shopping on Sunday, the coming Sunday they would buy ingredients for two different main dishes. When they got home from the store, they would prepare the ingredients for both meals, and put the ingredients for one meal into the Crock-Pot, turn it on, and go out and enjoy their day. Have what they made for dinner that night, and put the rest into freezable containers. The next morning before they went to work, they would put the ingredients for the second meal in the Crock-Pot, turn it on, and go to work. When they came home, dinner would be ready to dish out, and after dinner put the rest into freezable containers.

Then, on nights when they were "too tired" to fix a meal, instead of spending two hours, and $25-50 going out, pull one of the containers out of the freezer, heat it up, and have a nice and healthy meal at home, spend the evening relaxing and saving money that could pay for a nice vacation each year.

CROCK-POT WEALTH GROUP

While you can save money making meals on your own with a crock pot, it can be even more fun to get a group of friends together to "share a meal."

Find four friends who would be interested in participating in a "meal share program." Each makes a 5-quart Crock-Pot of something they like and fills five separate one quart containers. Then get together for an evening of fellowship and "exchange" what you each made.

You'll each have five different meals for your family while only preparing one yourself.

If you each saved $50 a week, each of you would save $2,600 / year. If you spend $600 of the savings for special "dinners out" during the year, you'd still have $2,000 a year to invest for the years ahead. And if you do this with people you'd spend time with anyway, you could do it for years and have as much fun as if you all went out to dinner - for a fraction of the cost.

CROCK-POT MEAL SHARING

Year	Invested	Cumulative Investment	With 7% MTE*
1	$2,000	$2,000	$140
2	$2,000	$4,140	$290
3	$2,000	$6,430	$450
4	$2,000	$8,880	$622
5	$2,000	$11,501	$805
....			
10	$2,000	$27,633	$1,934
....			
20	$2,000	$81,991	$5,739

MTE = **M**oney **T**ree **E**ffect (see Chapter "What's an MTE?")

> **"If you want to make good use of your time, you've got to know what's most important and then give it all you've got." - Lee Iacocca**

Dressing Up Baby

Babies really don't care where mom and dad buy their clothes. They don't care whether their clothes cost $3,000 / year at a designer boutique, or $500 / year from a thrift store (including cost of first cleaning).

And most babies grow so fast that many of the outfits are only worn a couple times before they are too small, so even clothing purchased used is usually in pretty good shape.

But if mom and dad saved even $1,500 a year buying clothes at thrift stores or consignment shops, savings could add up even if done for just the first five years.

DRESSING UP BABY

Year	Savings	Invested at 7%	7% MTE*
1	$1,500	$1,500	$105
2	$1,500	$3,105	$217
3	$1,500	$4,822	$338
4	$1,500	$6,660	$466
5	$1,500	$8,626	$604
.....			
16		$18,157	$1,271
.....			
18		$20,788	$1,455
.....			
21		$25,466	$1,783
.....			
30		$46,818	$3,277
.....			
40		$92,097	$6,447
.....			
50		$181,169	$12,682
.....			
55		$254,099	$17,787
.....			
60		$356,388	$24,947

*MTE = **M**oney **T**ree **E**ffect (see Chapter "What's an MTE?")

The ages displayed in the "Dressing up Baby" chart are not the standard "5-year" sequence provided on most tables in the book, but rather ages that often have significance in a child's or young adult's life.

For example, based on the assumptions used, at 16 there would be around $18,000 that could be used for a car. However, if those funds were left to grow until the child was 18, there would be over $20,000 accumulated that could be used for a senior trip, or maybe even pay for a year off to travel before starting college. Again, if instead left to grow, by 21, when this child might be ready to graduate from college, over $25,000 could be available to buy a house, fund a business, or pay off college loans. By age 55, when many who are working would like to be able to retire, or at least cut back on how much they work, more than a quarter million would have been accumulated, enough to withdraw more than $17,000 a year from that time on.

And remember, all this was created by investing $1,500 a year for just 5 years instead of buying nicer clothing for a child who is unlikely to know the difference.

Another idea if you have several friends who have children who are a little older: offer to buy their children's clothing for a price that might be more than they would get in tax savings from donating them to a charity, but that would enable you to buy at a low price from someone you know.

Is Community College Your Path to Greater Wealth?

Attending a 4-year university has some great benefits, but as more jobs don't require a 4-year degree, if your goal is to be financially independent, going to a community college for the first two years may be a wise use of both your time and money.

The Bureau of Labor Statistics (BLS) estimates of the 15-16 million jobs to be filled by 2022, 13 million or so will not require a degree, and many others will need only an associate (2-year) degree.

While a college degree increases the odds of being employed, how much they earn may greatly depend on WHAT their degree is in.

College degrees in science, technology, engineering and math (STEM) are projected to be both needed, and rewarded with higher salaries, but not every person has an interest in working in one of those fields. *NOTE: In "The Millionaire Mind," you can read stories of self-made multi-millionaires without college degrees, but most achieved their wealth through business ownership.*

Assume a potential employer only cares where your child graduated and his grades, and that costs for a 4-year university versus a 2-year community college were as show below:

Year	4-year university	Community college	Difference
1	$12,000	$3,000	$9,000
2	$12,840	$3,210	$9,630

The "Community College Savings" table illustrates potential wealth, as well as the potential annual income, that could be created through the years if the invested funds are assumed to earn 7% a year.

As this table illustrates, based on the assumptions used, by age 60 (end of year age 59) the savings from attending two years at a community college, then two years at a full university, instead of a 4-year college / university would be worth over $298,000 – enough to withdraw over $20,000 every year for the rest of their life.

Spending four years making friends and potential contacts, getting accustomed in the early years to the pace of a 4-year university and living on your own, definitely has benefits. The question is whether those potential benefits outweigh the potential illustrated by the table below.

COMMUNITY COLLEGE SAVINGS

End of year age	Year 1 invested at 7%	Year 2 invested at 7%	Total accumulated	7% MTE*
18	$9,630		$9,630	$674
19	$10,304	$9,630	$19,934	$1,395
20	$11,025	$10,304	$21,329	$1,493
.....				
25	$15,464	$14,452	$29,916	$2,094
......				
30	$21,689	$20,270	$41,958	$2,937
......				
35	$30,419	$28,429	$58,849	$4,119
......				
40	$42,665	$39,874	$82,538	$5,778
......				
45	$59,840	$55,925	$115,764	$8,104
......				
50	$83,928	$78,437	$162,365	$11,366
......				
55	$117,713	$110,013	$227,726	$15,941
....				
59	$154,298	$144,204	$298,502	$20,895

*MTE = **M**oney **T**ree **E**ffect (see Chapter "What's an MTE?")

What is important is to be able to compare the benefits you feel a four year university experience will bring, versus what the savings, invested, could be worth in the future to CHOOSE which is best for YOU.

Is Saving Money Costing You Wealth?

I read an article years ago that said there were four basic objectives people wanted to achieve as a result of spending money that I've found to be pretty realistic:

1. Increase pleasure / happiness / comfort
2. Reduce pain / frustration / aggravation / discomfort
3. Increase wealth
4. Reduce debt

I don't know about you, but I seem to get a $10 off $25, or $5 off $15 coupon at least once a month. Offer after offer to SAVE MONEY.

I readily admit sometimes I just can't resist, but I find generally what I end up buying is something I really don't need, and it ends up being given as a gift or silent auction item for a local fund-raiser.

If what you are buying on sale is something you truly want/need, do it. But if being able to work by CHOICE is one of your top goals, keep in mind that each dollar you spend on something you don't need could be invested and might bring you closer to that goal.

Bottom line if you decide the current benefit of spending money now exceeds the potential lifetime wealth that money invested might produce, then buy and enjoy.

All I would encourage you to do BEFORE COMPLETING YOUR PURCHASE, is to answer - for yourself - the following questions:

1. Is what you are planning to buy truly adding LONG TERM VALUE to your life?
2. One year from now, will the pleasure from what you are buying now be worth more – TO YOU – than the income that money could have generated for the rest of your life?

> ***"TO GET WHERE YOU WANT TO GO, YOU GENERALLY NEED TO KNOW WHERE YOU ARE."***
>
> from "*Better, Cheaper, Faster*"
> - by Michael Hammer and Lisa W. Hershman

Don't Be a Stuffy Person

I find a lot of the "stuff" I've bought through the years ended up gathering dust or donated to the local SPCA or other charity.

Fortunately for me, most of what I buy is already from the SPCA or another thrift store, so I don't have much invested (*which of course is how I try to rationalize it when I buy*), but any stuff you don't really use, regardless of how little it cost, ultimately is an obstacle to creating your personal wealth machine.

Here's an embarrassing personal example: Years ago, I asked my always well-dressed but thrift store shopping sister-in-law to take me shopping with her. I got hooked. I was "saving money" all the time. Then one day I heard a crash from my back room closet. A clothing bar had collapsed – trying to support seventy-two pairs of slacks. That may not seem like much, but I didn't wear slacks to work, and even though all seventy-two pairs probably cost less than five pairs at their original price, it was a real wake-up call to how easily even "bargains" can get out of hand.

My guess is that like me, you have stuff you've had for years that you haven't used, but you just KNOW if you give it away or donate it, THAT is when it will be needed.

Just a thought, but if you sell (or donate and get a tax deduction) half the stuff you haven't used for years, you could spend the profits/savings on things you actually need or want, or invest it to generate extra income to enjoy now or in the future.

Movies at Home with Friends

Suppose through their high school years, six friends go to the movies each weekend during the school year (30 weekends) and tickets, soda and popcorn cost $14 per person.

Now, suppose one of the friends, Sue, suggests instead of going to the theater on Saturday nights, they all get together at her house, everyone pitches in $4.00 to pay for renting two movies, and buying popcorn and sodas for everyone to share. That means each person would save $10 per weekend, or $300 a year.

If they did that all through high school, invested the savings and it earned 7% a year, by the time they graduated, each would have accumulated $1,332 which they could spend, or leave invested.

MOVIES AT HOME WITH FRIENDS

Year	Invested	Accumulated at 7%
1	$300	$300
2	$300	$621
3	$300	$964
4	$300	$1,332

As they were getting ready to graduate, Sue suggested it might be fun if they all left the money invested, and at their 40th class reunion use the money they had accumulated to do something fun together. Since the goal was to use the money for the 40th reunion, it would remain invested for 39 years and withdrawn at the start of year 40.

Sue then showed them the table labeled "40th Reunion Fund" that she had created.

Her friends were delightfully surprised to learn if they left the money invested (earning 7% a year), each would have $18,000 to spend on a special 40th reunion gathering.

40th REUNION FUND

Years after	Investment	Accumulated at 7%
1	$1,332	$1,425
2		$1,525
3		$1,632
4		$1,746
5		$1,868
.....		
10		$2,620
.....		
15		$3,675
.....		
20		$5,154
.....		
25		$7,229
.....		
30		$10,140
.....		
35		$14,221
36		$15,217
37		$16,282
38		$17,422
39		$18,641

Not a bad benefit from spending time with good friends sharing a meal and watching movies at home.

Old Mother Hubbard

There's a children's poem about Old Mother Hubbard, who "went to the cupboard to find her poor doggy a bone. But when she got there, the cupboard was bare, and so the poor doggie had none."

A study from the Johns Hopkins Center for a Livable Future (CLF) found 31 to 40 percent of the American food supply goes to waste, primarily in homes, stores and restaurants. The estimated cost in 2010 was $161.6 billion annually. According to the U.S. Census, there were about 116 million U.S. households in 2010. That means the average food wasted per household was around $1,400.

I love saving money. Problem is, sometimes trying to save money actually costs money.

When I moved into my house it had a big pantry and two refrigerators. Then I bought a freezer since I was planning to do a lot of entertaining. Needless to say, I didn't want an empty cupboard when someone came by, so I made sure everything was generally full. I figured I was doing good because most of the food I bought on sale.

What I discovered is just because I bought something on sale, didn't mean I actually saved money because virtually all food has a limited useful life. Unless you have a very large family or entertain a lot, odds are filling a pantry can lead to a lot of wasted food.

In my case, as the expiration date neared, I donated the food to some local charities, but I now realize it may be better to buy as needed, even if it's not on sale, than to have so much food that many items reach their "use by" date before they are needed and end up getting thrown out or given away.

You may be a lot better at this than I am, but in case you don't regularly go through your refrigerator or pantry / cupboards, give it a try and see how much is actually out of date. You may be as surprised as I was at how much was well past its recommended "use by" date.

As a suggestion: Plan out a weekly menu, preferably on the day the grocery store advertising flyers come out so if you want, you can plan your week's menu around what is on sale that week, but closely check the "use by" date and only buy what you realistically expect to use by that date. Otherwise, what you are essentially doing is throwing MONEY away.

Where Were You 20 Years Ago?

Years ago when I was doing retirement seminars a frequent comment at the end was: "Where were you 20 years ago when I really could have used this information?"

Many young people I've talked with about saving say they're going to wait because they have plenty of time, don't have much money now, and will have more money later and will be better able to save.

But too often, as income increases "needs" increase faster than income. If a "pay yourself first " habit is not developed early in ones paycheck receiving years, it is likely to be far more difficult to AFFORD that habit later, and there may not be enough available cash flow to make "catching up" possible.

For example, assuming your investments earned 7% a year, if your goal was to accumulate $1 million in 20 years, you would need to invest $24,390 each of those 20 years. But if you had 40 years to reach that same $1 million goal, you would only need to invest $5,131 a year.

You can use Appendix F to calculate the investment needed for other investment returns or years. For example, to calculate the FIXED annual investment needed to accumulate $1 million in 20 years if you assume your investments will earn 7% a year, you would use Table IIA-0, find the value where 20 years and 7% Rate of Return (ROR) intersect (value = 41.00). You would then divide that value into your goal amount ($1,000,000). The Result, $24,390.

A thought to keep in mind:

Each dollar you SPEND is income for someone else. Each dollar you SAVE could be future income for yourself.

The Wisdom of Others

I've found through the years that some of my best ideas come from others.

Following are three memorable statements that you might find helpful as well:

About LIFE

From a salesman friend after I made a statement about a project of his I was working on: "Ilene," he said, "do you know what you are doing when you "assume" anything?" ... "You are making an A_ _ out of "U" and "ME."

Silly, perhaps. But far too often, Accurate. Do not "assume" your future is taken care of by programs like social security and company pensions. A lot of people who made similar assumptions are finding their "golden years" aren't so golden after all, and that their life revolves around waiting for that next check to arrive just to pay their basic bills.

About RETIREMENT

From a 21-year-old friend who was wise beyond her age in this respect: "Retirement is a REWARD, not a PUNISHMENT." But I would also add that if someone has not planned adequately for it financially, it could SEEM like a punishment when they can afford to do little more than survive from day to day and year to year.

About FINANCIAL PLANNING

From the personnel manager of our local school board, probably the most astute remark:

"We spend 25 years preparing for our working career, yet we often spend only a year, or less, preparing for our retirement." Most people devote more time to planning a lifetime of vacations than they do planning their vacation of a lifetime.

The Eighth Wonder of the World...

"Compound interest is the eighth wonder of the world. He who understands it, earns it ... he who doesn't ... pays it."
Albert Einstein

The sad fact is that many Americans do not understand the concept of compound interest. And many clients have told me they never learned about it in school.

To see the incredible power of compound interest at work, consider a story about Benjamin Franklin.*

As the story goes, When Franklin died in 1790, he left a gift worth around $4,500 in current dollars to each of his two favorite cities, Boston and Philadelphia. The money was to be invested earning 5% / year. After 100 years, each city was to take 75% of the funds that had accumulated to use for public works, and leave the remaining 25% invested (assuming 5% per year) for another 100 years. At the end of that next 100 years, each city would get about 25% of the money and their respective states would get the rest. Had Boston and Philly followed Franklin's wishes, they would have each had nearly $20,000,000 in their funds at the end of the 200 years.

The chart "Ben Franklin's Gift" shows the year end value of Franklin's $4,500 invested per his instructions at year 10, then at the end of each 20th year.

BEN FRANKLIN'S GIFT

Year	Invested	End of year value	25% left at year 100	Balance at 5% / year
1	$4,500	$4,725		
10		$7,330		
20		$11,940		
40		$31,680		
60		$84,056		
80		$223,025		
100		$591,751	$147,938	
120				$392,523
140				$1,041,481
160				$2,763,359
180				$7,332,015
200				$19,454,019

And imagine what that would be if there were no withdrawal at the 100th year anniversary!!

I know. You don't want to wait 100 to 200 years to stop working, but here is a true story of two wise parents and how they ensured their children had to option to stop working at an age many of their children's peers would still need to work even to maintain a modest lifestyle.

They set up accounts for their children when their son was 7 and daughter 5. When the son was 24, he came to meet with me to learn a little more about investing (If only more 24 year olds were as wise!!).

At that time, the account his parents had set up was worth approximately $440,000. A review of past statements showed about $60,000 had been invested between 1990 and 1993.

He already had a job, and a business, and no plans to use this money for his living expenses, so I did some calculations to show what that money could be worth at different rates of return 35 years later, when he would be almost 60 and want to spend more time fishing than working. Here were the results (rounded to nearest $1,000):

- If the $440,000 earned 2%, it would be worth $880,000.
- If the $440,000 earned 4%, it would be worth $1,736,000.
- If the $440,000 earned 6%, it would be worth $3,382,000.
- If the $440,000 earned 8%, it would be worth $6,505,000.

And while I would never, EVER use a return of 10% or 12% for planning, I did show him the following calculations as well:

- If the $440,000 earned 10%, it would be worth $12,365,000.
- If the $440,000 earned 12%, it would be worth $23,232,000.

Even though it won't buy as much in 35 years, I thought that was a pretty incredible legacy to leave a child. To accumulate $6.5 million, even assuming a net 10% a year, he would have had to invest $24,000 each and every year of those 35 years. And what a great lesson to implement for HIS children and replicate that legacy.

My parting suggestion: go home and give your mom and dad a great big hug!!

> ***Time and compound interest can be a great partner in accumulating wealth.***

**To read the full story on this, Google "Benjamin Franklin compound interest."*

Make Room For Wealth

One of the biggest purchases most people make is buying a place to live, be it a house, condo, or even a boat.

Suppose you were considering two hypothetical homes. They are in the same neighborhood, so children would go to the same school. One is 2,000 square feet (SF) and costs $200,000, the other is 1,800 square feet (SF) and costs $180,000. A difference of 200 square feet and $20,000.

If the 30-year rate on a fixed mortgage is 6.5%, monthly payments (rounded to the nearest dollar) for principal and interest on the 2,000 SF home would be $1,266 ($15,192 / year), and for the 1,800 SF home would be $1013 ($12,154 / year).

Assuming you could afford either of the homes, if you CHOSE to purchase the smaller home, the difference in principal and interest payments would be $3,038 per year. Further assume you would invest the difference and it would earn 7% / year.

If you bought the smaller house and kept it for 30 years, invested the difference in payments and those invested savings earned 7% a year, the wealth created by living in the smaller home and investing the difference in payments would be over $285,000, which at 7% would allow you to withdraw more than $20,000 a year, "forever." (See table"Room for Wealth.")

The CHOICE is yours, you can choose to have 200 SF more to live in, or have the potential to accumulate over a QUARTER MILLION DOLLARS to spend on other things. And that's just the savings on principal and interest payments. Assuming taxes and insurance total 1% of the purchase price, taxes and insurance would be $2,000 / year on the bigger house, and $1,800 / year on the smaller one. A savings of $200 / year in savings that could be invested, or used to pay for parties at your smaller, wealth-building home. Use the tables in the appendix to do the math on what $200 a year, invested instead of spent, could build up to over the years.

ROOM FOR WEALTH

Year	Savings	Invested at 7%	7% MTE*
1	$3,038	$3,038	**$213**
2	$3,038	$6,289	**$440**
3	$3,038	$9,767	**$684**
4	$3,038	$13,489	**$944**
5	$3,038	$17,471	**$1,223**
6	$3,038	$21,732	**$1,521**
7	$3,038	$26,291	**$1,840**
8	$3,038	$31,169	**$2,182**
9	$3,038	$36,389	**$2,547**
10	$3,038	$41,974	**$2,938**
:::			
15	$3,038	$76,342	**$5,344**
:::::			
20	$3,038	$124,544	**$8,718**
:::::			
25	$3,038	$192,151	**$13,451**
:::::			
30	$3,038	$286,972	**$20,088**

*MTE = **M**oney **T**ree **E**ffect (see Chapter "What's an MTE?")

NOTE: For those readers closer to retirement, even if you only invested the savings for 15 years before you started using it to generate income, you would have accumulated over $75,000 – enough with that money earning 7% a year to withdraw over $5,000 a year, year after year with the principal left intact.

Make College Living Pay Real Dividends

I don't know about you, but my college years were some of the best (read: minimal responsibility, maximum freedom from parental oversight) of my life. Granted, my grades weren't exactly what my dad was looking for, but I learned enough to get a decent job, had lots of friends, and lived a great life for minimal expense. In fact, the only real expenses I had were tuition, books, and housing costs. And with five of us sharing a three bedroom apartment, pizza parties and cooking with friends a normal form of weekend entertainment, movies and plays at student rates - the cost of living was not high (of course, neither was our income!)

From what I've seen of college students today, they can live just as inexpensively (adjusted for inflation) as I did 40 years earlier if they are willing to live a similar lifestyle.

Sadly, many new graduates go on a spending spree when they start making "real" money. But what if they didn't? The following example assumes a salary of $37,000, taxes of $7,000, $15,000 a year for living expenses for just 2 or 3 years, and the remaining $15,000 invested each year.

POOR NOW ..... RICH LATER

Age	Invested	Earning 7% a yr.	7% / yr. MTE*	Invested	Earning 7% a yr.	7% a yr. MTE*
22	$15,000	$15,000	$1,050	$15,000	$15,000	$1,050
23	$15,000	$31,050	$2,174	$15,000	$31,050	$2,174
24		$33,224	$2,326	$15,000	$48,224	$3,376
25		$35,549	$2,488		$51,599	$3,612
.....						
30		$49,860	$3,490		$72,370	$5,066
.....						
40		$98,080	$6,866		$142,363	$9,965
.....						
50		$192,937	$13,506		$280,049	$19,603
.....						
60		$379,536	$26,568		$550,898	$38,563
......						
65		$532,318	$37,262		$772,663	$54,086

*MTE = **M**oney **T**ree **E**ffect (see Chapter "What's an MTE?")

And unless your college years were a lot different than mine, living the "college life" for a couple years after graduation shouldn't be much of a sacrifice ... you might even find it's a lot more fun to share a place with friends and party at home than to be on your own – even without the considering how this lifestyle could help you create a pretty nice potential "money tree orchard" to help support you in later years.

And if having to "give up" $15,000 of your income is just too much, the following table shows the results of investing $6,000 / year for five years, or $10,000 for three years. The same $30,000, just spread out over a few more years.

POOR NOW ... RICH A LITTLE LATER

Age	Invested	Earning 7% a yr.	Invested	Earning 7% a yr.	Invested	Earning 7% a yr.
22	$6,000	$6,000	$10,000	$10,000	$15,000	$15,000
23	$6,000	$12,420	$10,000	$20,700	$15,000	$31,050
24	$6,000	$19,289	$10,000	$32,149		$33,224
25	$6,000	$26,640		$34,399		$35,549
26	$6,000	$34,504		$36,807		$38,038
:::::		$36,920		$39,384		$40,700
30		$45,228		$48,247		$49,860
:::::						
40		$88,971		$94,909		$98,080
:::::						
50		$175,019		$186,701		$192,937
:::::						
60		$344,289		$367,269		$379,536
:::::						
65		$482,883		$515,114		$532,318

It's YOUR CHOICE, but if you consider the wealth created by age 65 based on a total of $30,000 invested as illustrated in the "Poor Now ... Rich a little later" table above.

- $482,883 at age 65 would have a 7% MTE* = $33,801
- $515,114 at age 65 would have a 7% MTE* = $36,058
- $532,318 at age 65 would have a 7% MTE* = $37,262

* MTE = **M**oney **T**ree **E**ffect (see Chapter "What's an MTE?")

If you consider lifetime income of more than $30,000 a year to spend in exchange for postponing the immediate "rewards" of a higher income, you might agree there's a lot to be said for a couple years of the "poor life" to create the foundation for a "rich life" later on.

If comedian Henny Youngman *(to whom I saw it attributed)* **is correct that "The easiest way to remain poor is to pretend to be rich." Could it also be that, "One of the easiest ways to become rich is to pretend to be poor – at least for a few years?"**

Ownership Can be an Obstacle to Wealth

You've probably seen T-shirts and bumper stickers stating "He who dies with the most toys, wins." There's also one that reminds us that "He with the most toys, still dies."

But a more accurate proclamation might be: "he with the most toys is likely to be unable to afford to retire while friends with fewer toys are enjoying life without needing to work."

"Toy" ownership may be good for the ego, but it is often devastating for the pocketbook.

One problem with being a financial adviser is I tend to analyze the financial benefits versus costs of many things others don't.

My boyfriend often laughs at me when I compute the annual income of different things I could buy. A friend recently commented on my choice of car and suggested surely I could afford a more expensive car than I had purchased. I explained the car I bought gets me back and forth to work just fine, and likely costs $10,000 less a little spiffier car. $10,000 invested earning 7% a year would generate $700 each year. Since my car generally sits around doing nothing but collecting dust 22 out of most 24 hour days, I would rather spend $700 a year on other things than a fancier car.

Ultimately, focusing on priorities can help you make "wealthier" choices. If a more expensive car wasn't going to help me toward my ultimate goal of financial independence, why spend more when something less expensive would do what I needed.

If YOUR goal is to have the use of an object, but also want to maximize your wealth, you might consider analyzing the "rent versus buy" option on a "cost per hour used" basis to see which is best for you.

For example, a client looking to buy a motor home had been advised they were better off renting than pulling money out of their investments to buy it. But they weren't asked an important question: how much were they going to use the motor home?

Had they planned to use it just a couple weeks a year, that would have been good advice. But since they were planning to be traveling by motor home 6 months of the year, this couple was better off buying the motor home, particularly since the husband was really good at fixing things.

Another friend could easily afford to keep his $200,000 houseboat. But he planned to spend 9 months a year where the boat was completely impractical. We did the numbers. To have the boat docked and maintained would cost $500 - $1,000 a month. Selling the boat and investing the money at 7% would produce annual income of $14,000 a year. Adding in the dockage/maintenance costs (that would have been paid if they kept the boat) produced a net "income" of $20,000 - $25,000 a year. With that money, he could lease a houseboat when he wanted, hire a captain to run it while he partied, and leave it for someone else to clean up when he was done. He decided to sell it.

Another client had a condo in the mountains she and her husband bought years before. He had passed away, but she kept the place because she had friends there she golfs with. But she was now in her 70s, and it was a 10-hour drive up there. Meanwhile, it cost her $17,000 a year to keep and maintain it.

When we talked about it, she focused on the emotional attachment and the friends she golfed with. Needless to say, I looked at it from a "cost / benefit" perspective for the 3 months she generally used it each year.

Here was my analysis: She could rent a nice place nearby for $3,000 a month, so if she went for 3 months, total cost would be $9,000 a year - $8,000 a year less than owning her condo. When I brought that up, she said all her friends had told her she was welcome to stay with them, so if she wanted, she could spend time with her friends, her costs might be $1,000 a month to treat her host to dinner, pay for their golfing, and buy a thank you gift.

After our discussion she decided on an acceptable selling price. I was so happy when 6 months later she called to tell me it was sold and she felt an incredible weight had been lifted off her shoulders.

She still goes up occasionally to golf with friends, but since she sold the condo, she has taken trips with friends to golf courses in other areas, taken a cruise to Europe with her daughter, and other travels. Even better - the $100,000 she was able to put in the bank gave her peace of mind, and instead of spending $17,000 a year maintaining a seldom used condo, she could spend it on golf, travel, gifts, or whatever else she wanted to do.

You may still prefer to own, but if you decide to do a "rent versus buy" comparison, here is my suggestion to do it with a "wealthy mindset."

1. Calculate the likely number of years you will own it and the total cost of ownership - initial cost PLUS annual expenses to own and maintain.

2. Calculate the hours/days, you are likely to use it during that total period of time.

3. Divide the total cost by the total hours/days of use.

4. Compare that per hour/day cost to what it would cost to rent per hour/day.

> ***"ACCESS IS A PRIVILEGE. OWNERSHIP IS A BURDEN."***
> – *"The Middle-Class Millionaire"*
> by Russ Alan Prince and Lewis Schiff

Pennies From Heaven?

T. Harv Eker, NY Times No. 1 Best-selling author of "Secrets of the Millionaire Mind"™ says, when he was cool and poor, he would never stoop to pick up a penny, but once rich and "hokey," he not only stopped to pick up the pennies, but he would, out loud, thank "the universe" for making him a money magnet.

What I have discovered through the years is many people don't think about time and money in the same way I do, so perhaps the stories that follow could be useful to you in creating your own path to greater wealth.

Years ago, I was standing in line at the post office waiting to mail a letter. The woman in front of me had taken out her wallet, since she was next in line to be served. In the process, she dropped a penny. She looked down at it, then walked forward as "next" was called.

Here were my thoughts: There are 60 seconds in a minute, and 60 minutes in an hour. That means there are 3,600 seconds in an hour. If it took two seconds of "work" to pick up that penny, that's the equivalent of earning $18 / hour.

Yes, I know, you can't find a penny on the ground every couple seconds. That's a typical response when I tell that story. Maybe that's because most jobs are no longer based on "piecework," but on hours worked.

I never realized this "disconnect" between time and money earned until a meeting with a client's friend who invented a useful product with a potential market of millions. He had been marketing it during the day because his "real job" was at night. Then his employer moved him to the day shift, and suddenly he could not call on potential customers during their business hours. My clients suggested he come to see me.

I asked him how much profit he made on each piece and how much he made at his job. Then calculated he would need to sell 55,000 pieces a year to generate as much in profits as he earned at his job. He looked at me and said "If I have time to go to a couple trades shows, I could do that in two months."

My response was simple: "*Then my question to you is do you want to work two months or twelve months for the same amount of money.*" He decided if sales went well during Christmas he would quit his job (his wife worked so it wouldn't put them under financial strain) and run his business full time. When I called him four months later, he said he had already made as much profit as he earned at his job the prior year, and now his goal was to make that much in a month.

A client enjoyed going to garage sales on weekends and finding things to sell on Ebay. One day she was telling me how miserable she was at her job. Knowing about her Ebay selling, I asked how much she could make per hour if she really worked her Ebay site, and how much she made at her job. It turned out if she spent two days a week really working her Ebay site, she could make as much as she made at a job she didn't enjoy. Family issues prevented her from working that idea, but thousands of people have fun and make money via their Ebay or Amazon "stores."

This is just a thought, but as I learned at the "Millionaire Mind Intensive" seminar, it may be "hokey" to pick up pennies, but what do you have to lose by spending a few seconds each morning visualizing yourself as a "money magnet" and telling "the universe" you are open to new ideas and ready to receive all the opportunities it might be willing to send your way.

You never know what you might just receive in response.

It never hurts to ask for help. Even if the Universe doesn't answer, someone else might offer you an idea that becomes your personal "ticket to wealth."

Put it in the Drawer

Every few weeks, I get either a catalog or packet of items from companies like Oriental Trading, Collections, Starcrest, etc. My latest from Starcrest was full of 148 sheets with some really useful products, at reasonable prices. PRETTY TEMPTING!! Especially when you only have to buy four items to get "free shipping" and a free gift!

I've actually bought a lot of useful items through them that I hadn't seen in stores that make great and affordable gifts for others, or items I can use. Many of the things I buy are things that can make life easier for my mom (who is 93), and she is always amazed at what I find. She can use the magnifying eyeglasses and have both hands free to do her stained glass. When I realized a client was having real trouble seeing the numbers on her phone, I bought her a pair as well and she said they were fabulous. Talk about an affordable way to bring joy. I also found some great "steamers" for the microwave that eliminate spattering because they have vents. And I found a little tool for mom that cost $6.00 that made it easy to open pop-top cans that can be difficult for many seniors to do. But what I began to realize is "instant gratification" led me to buying things I didn't really need. Not exactly helping me accumulate wealth for the years ahead.

My solution: Instead of placing an order, I pull out the pages of stuff I think I want, put them in the envelope, and put the envelope with my "desired purchases" in a drawer. I've found when I look at them a month later, most of what I had considered buying was stuff I really didn't need, or even want. It was just that "rush of desire" to buy all those seemingly great things I felt I just couldn't live without. What I try to do now is limit my order to less than $100 per three months. And I really try to know WHO will be the recipient of an item before I place the order.

With the internet and daily doses of "buy it today and get all this extra stuff and you can return it if you don't like it" ads on TV, it can be a lot harder to "put it in the drawer," but I'm confident if you truly want to accumulate wealth, you will consider doing like I do and write down the item and phone number, put THAT in a drawer, and see if a month later it really is something you just can't live without.

And one other thought. Write down the amount you planning to spend. The next day go to the bank and take out that amount, IN CASH, and put it in a safe place. At the end of the month, count how much you would have spent, divide it by 20 for a rough estimate of what that money, invested at 5% a year, could generate year after year in income for you. It provides a long-term perspective to help counter some of the need we all have for more immediate gratification.

Leftover Night

I don't know about you, but when I find time to clean out the refrigerator, I usually find at least one container full of something totally unidentifiable other than as green mold. YUCK!

But after reading a survey by the Natural Resources Defense Council about wasted food, I realized that could add up to a lot of extra income to be enjoyed instead of being thrown in the trash.

Then I remembered when I was growing up, one of our favorite "dinner nights" was what mom called "leftover night." I don't recall if it was usually on a weekend, or just whenever she saw food piling up in the refrigerator, but I do remember it was a fun night because you could pick and choose what you wanted to eat from what was left over from the prior week or two.

I know when I have a party, I generally have perfectly good food left over that I freeze. In fact, as the food sponsor for a recent Chamber Ambassadors meeting, I introduced my fellow Ambassadors to leftover night by bringing stuff from my New Years, and Super Bowl parties from earlier this year. All the food was gone, and I got several thumbs-up, so I was able to make space in my freezer and feed a dozen people using leftovers from earlier parties.

Here's an idea you might find fun to do when you find your fridge or freezer full of leftovers: invite some friends over for a night of games, watching a movie, having some good conversation, and have a "clean the fridge / freezer" night.

Suppose with some better food planning and making meals from leftovers, you could save $1,000 a year on food costs.

And further suppose that you invested that money and it earned 7% a year. If you did that for just 10 years, as you can see in the "Leftover Night" table that follows, the money you saved and invested could generate almost $1,000 a year, year after year to spend on going out to dinner or other things you would enjoy doing.

LEFTOVER NIGHT

Year	Saved	Invested at 7%	7% MTE*
1	$1,000	$1,000	$70
2	$1,000	$2,070	$145
3	$1,000	$3,215	$225
4	$1,000	$4,440	$311
5	$1,000	$5,751	$403
6	$1,000	$7,153	$501
7	$1,000	$8,654	$606
8	$1,000	$10,260	$718
9	$1,000	$11,978	$838
10	$1,000	$13,816	$967
.....			
15	$1,000	$25,129	$1,759
.....			
20	$1,000	$40,995	$2,870
.....			
25	$1,000	$63,249	$4,427
.....			
30	$1,000	$94,461	$6,612

*MTE = **M**oney **T**ree **E**ffect (see Chapter "What's an MTE?")

And remember, you don't have to do this for 30 years! You can stop at any time, and if you look at the 7% MTE column, the value shown is the potential annual income your "Leftover Investment Fund" could generate each year, "forever," assuming a continued average 7% investment return.

> **"Waste not, want not"** is a phrase I heard a lot when we were kids. One website I found said the earliest recorded use of this was in 1576, when the exact phrase was **"willful waste makes woeful want."** Seems either of those phrases posted on your mirror to read each day is a wealthy idea.

Easy Come, Easy Go

While wealth can bring great happiness to those who are already happy, sadly, wealth, particularly sudden wealth, can actually lead to unhappiness, even early death.

Surveys have found many people who receive a lump sum (insurance settlement, lottery, etc.) have used, (or lost) it all within five years. It's so common, it's been given a name: "Sudden Wealth Syndrome."

I believe at least one of the reasons a lump sum can be "lost" so quickly is many who receive one don't realize just how quickly even large amounts can disappear if not managed carefully.

I recommend you check out the Vanderbilt family. When Cornelius Vanderbilt died in 1877 (on the same day and month that I was born !!), he was worth more than $100 million. At a family reunion in the 1970s, not one of the 120 attending was still a millionaire. (Google "Vanderbilt fortune gone" for the details.)

It's amazing how such a fortune could disappear in just 100 years, but there continue to be stories about winners of multi-million dollar lotteries, and how sudden wealth turned their lives upside down.

Consider the following real life examples:

I had the opportunity to work with two teenagers, one 16, and one 13 who received lump sum settlements from car accidents. Both were offered the same advice, both had parents at our meeting.

The 16 year old received $100,000. He said he was going to use some for school, but invest the rest. Instead, he bought a new Jeep Grand Cherokee. His uncle didn't know where the rest went but knew it was gone in two years. The 13 year old received $30,000. She invested the full settlement (perhaps the threat of bodily harm from her mother had something to do with it (just kidding). She used the money (and what it had earned) for school and down payment on a house, but I thought you might find it interesting to calculate what that $30,000 could have been worth in the following years.

Using Table FVS-1 in Appendix A, and assuming a 7% per year return, you should get the following answers:

- 10 years later it would be worth $59,010
- 30 years later it would be worth $228,360
- 50 years later it would be worth $883,710, enough to generate $61,860 each year after assuming a continued 7% a year investment return.

Had the 16 year old spent $60,000 for college, but invested the remaining $40,000 he received and it earned 7% a year, 50 years later when he was age 66 he would have accumulated more than $1.1 million.

Sadly, you can find many stories on the internet about lottery "losers," but the story about the potential harm "sudden wealth" can create that I will always remember is the one of Jack Whittaker. He won a $315 million Powerball jackpot in 2002 and was broke in four years. What makes his story particularly sad, besides the personal tragedies he suffered, is at the time he won this jackpot, he was president of his construction company and already worth over $15 million, so he obviously had SOME idea of how to manage wealth.

If he had invested $200 million of his winnings in 30-year government bonds (which at the time were paying over 5%), and spent the other $115 million, he could have had income of $10 million, every year for 30 years, and still had the $200 million left 30 years later.

Two great books on "WEALTH" are Dr. Thomas Stanley's "The Millionaire Next Door," and "The Millionaire Mind." I recommend them because they can help the reader understand the difference between INCOME, and WEALTH - between those who are INCOME affluent, and those who are BALANCE SHEET affluent.

Robert Kiyosaki addresses this concept in his "cash flow quadrant." Those on the left side of his cash flow diagram may be "income" affluent, but those on the right side of his diagram are often balance sheet affluent.

The primary difference is the "income" affluent can become poor very quickly if their source of income disappears. The "balance sheet" affluent have a source of income that does not depend on being able to work, or having to be in a particular place at a particular time to have income added to their bank account.

If you are more concerned about what others think of you than your own future and that of your loved ones, you may find accumulating wealth could be difficult. But if you care more about your future and that of your loved ones than what others (that 20-30 years later you can't remember) think, then I believe you can learn to think like a millionaire, and perhaps become one yourself.

Bottom line: The key to creating a personal wealth machine is to not just accumulate wealth, but to know how to manage that wealth. In the wrong hands, money won't buy happiness, or even peace of mind. As you create your own "fortune," perhaps the most important thing to keep in mind is when money controls you, instead of you controlling it, the end result may be misery instead of happiness, and stress instead of peace of mind.

Should you find yourself in possession of "sudden wealth," first, Google "lottery losers" for some sad but true stories. Then consider the following "system" that might help you avoid "sudden wealth syndrome" and provide the opportunity to enjoy increasing annual income in the years following.

1. Take 10% of whatever "sudden wealth" you receive. Do not invest it. Do not use it to pay off outstanding debt. Spend it on something that will make you smile ... and hopefully be a source of ongoing good memories.

2. If you have outstanding debt, take another 10-20% and use it to pay off debt. If not enough to pay it all off, make a list of debts in order of interest rates and pay off what you can in that order.

3. Invest the remaining 70-80% with at least half in investments that will produce current income, and use half each year's income to pay down debt until the debt is gone.

4. Of income produced each year, reinvest 25% back into income producing investments.

While nothing can guarantee this money will last as long as you do, this system can greatly increase the likelihood at least part of the lump sum you received will become a source of ongoing income. It may even be enough for you to live your "dream lifestyle" for the remainder of your life.

> ***"Wealth is what you accumulate,***
> ***not what you spend."***
>
> *"The Millionaire Next Door"*
>
> – Thomas Stanley

Play Tourist in a City Near You

You may have seen or heard the term "Staycation." Some hotels and tourist spots have used it in their advertising. What they are basically promoting is that you play "tourist" in a city near where you live so that you can easily get there, generally in less than an hour or two.

For example, I live near several places – Disney World, Universal Studios, Cocoa Beach and Daytona Beach - that millions of people spend thousands of dollars to come and visit for a week. When we feel the need to get away, we can pack up on a Saturday morning, drive 40 minutes to Cocoa Beach or Daytona Beach, eat lunch at a nice restaurant, check into the hotel and go for a swim, a walk on the beach, or visit some local "tourist spots," then go to dinner, or out to a show, just as if we were on vacation, then come home Sunday afternoon.

We've only been "gone" about 36 hours, but it feels like much more. No dogs to walk, no phones to answer, no beds to make. For little more than $100-$250 we've had a nice little vacation without a week of work to catch up on.

While not everyone is fortunate enough to have a Disney World or Cocoa Beach just a short drive away, throughout the country there are hundreds of neat places to visit within an hour drive for many people that others consider worthwhile vacation destinations. So instead of taking a vacation far away, consider being a tourist in your home town or someplace nearby every other year, and save what you would have otherwise spent if you had taken a vacation that required the added cost of buying airline tickets, renting a car, and so on.

Suppose the total cost of a typical week vacation for you and your family costs $1400 ($200 / day). Now suppose you stay at home, but spend the day visiting the same places the tourists visit and you save (i.e.: didn't spend) for that vacation. And you did this every OTHER year for five years.

By traveling close to home off and on for a couple years, not only would you learn more about your "back yard," but you'd have extra money to finance other vacations in future years.

TAKING A STAY-CATION

Year	Saved	Invested at 7%	7% MTE*
1	$900.00	$900	$63
2		$963	$67
3	$900.00	$1,930	$135
4		$2,066	$145
5	$900.00	$3,110	$218
.....			
10		$4,362	$305
.....			
15		$6,118	$428
.....			
20		$8,581	$601
.....			
25		$12,035	$842

ROR = Rate of return

*MTE = **M**oney **T**ree **E**ffect (see Chapter "What's an MTE?")

A Great Wedding Gift

Sue and Sam are both 22 and engaged to be married. Because they are both out of college and working, their parents felt they should contribute to their wedding, but offered to split the cost of the wedding with them. Each couple was to contribute $20,000 for a total of $60,000.

Their parents also gave them a CHOICE. If they decided to only spend $20,000, they would still keep the parents $40,000.

Sam was fine with that, but Sue had her heart set on a big, fancy wedding, so Sam's parents showed Sue the following:

A GREAT WEDDING GIFT

Age	Wedding gift	Invested at 7%	7% MTE*
22	$40,000	$42,800	$2,996
.....			
25		$52,432	$3,670
.....			
30		$73,538	$5,148
.....			
40		$144,661	$10,126
....			
50		$284,570	$19,920

*MTE = **M**oney **T**ree **E**ffect (see Chapter "What's an MTE?")

They explained if Sam and Sue invested the parents $40,000 and it earned 7% a year, by the time they were 30, they could start withdrawing more than $5,000 each and every year to spend on whatever they wanted as a "wedding gift" to themselves. If they delayed taking withdrawals until they were 50, they could take out almost $20,000 each year for the rest of their lives to spend on whatever they wanted to do, all as a gift to themselves for choosing a less expensive wedding.

Book Review

MONEY IS MY FRIEND

by Phil Laut

(NOTE: Many of the ideas in this book are similar to those in "The Richest Man in Babylon," but with a more contemporary perspective.)

I originally read this around 30 years ago, and didn't realize until recently re-reading it how much of it I had incorporated into my discussions with, and recommendations to, clients through the years.

I think a key lesson of this book is in the first line:

"The purpose of this book is to eliminate poverty in the world and to make abundant living socially acceptable."

Years ago, I had boat bags made as a client gift that included this definition of Financial Independence:

"Being able to do what you want, when you want, with whom you want, without having to work for it."

I still think that's a good definition, but I also like an idea Mr. Laut included in this book: That "Financial Freedom" is not only about what you CAN do, but also that you don't have to give up / sacrifice doing something you would like to do because you can't afford to do it.

Following are some points I particularly thought worth sharing:

- Only you can give power to negative emotions, by clinging to them.

- All the education you receive and improvements you make in life serve only to make you more productive to someone else's purpose unless you have a clear sense of your OWN purpose.

- A key to financial success is to view money in a positive light. To find peace with being wealthy. To not feel shame because you have more than someone else (odds are strong there are others who have more than you do and they are not ashamed by it).

- "Poverty consciousness" is often the result of how our parents talked about or acted around money. His affirmations for this are particularly worth reviewing. I particularly like his affirmation with regard to how your wealth contributes not only to your "aliveness," but to the aliveness of others that know you.

- "Mindset" is a key tool. Many people with great potential sabotage their own success. You may have also heard this concept called the "laws of attraction" – that we attract to ourselves what we are. That if we don't feel good about ourselves, we attract people who don't feel good about THEMselves.

- In the book, Mr. Laut recommends establishing seven different savings accounts. Because it can be expensive to set up separate accounts these days, I recommend having a card file that details how much of one (combined) account belongs in each category and use those balances. Two accounts in particular I've incorporated into my own recommendations are the Financial Independence account - which I call my "splurge" account, and the Millionaire's savings account, which I recommend as a client's Investment accounts.

Change Your Future

Clients have told me the change they saved through the year has been used to buy a set of golf clubs, pay for Christmas gifts, or pay for a long weekend away to relax.

With so many people using debit cards, the amount of change someone today is likely to have in their pocket may not be as much as in the past so this idea may no longer work for many readers, but let's suppose your "change" averages 55 cents a day. That adds up to $200 a year.

Now try this: Using Table FVA-0 in Appendix C, calculate how much $200 a year invested at different rates would be worth in 20 years, and in 30 years (HINT: because the table assumes an investment of $1,000 / year, an investment of $200 a year would use a multiplier of $200 / $1000 = .2).

DYING BROKE MAY BE GREAT, BUT BECOMING BROKE BEFORE YOU DIE SELDOM IS.

Answers:

Percentage used	20 years	30 years
2%	$ 4,859	$ 8,113
4%	$ 5,956	$ 11,217
6%	$ 7,357	$ 15,812
8%	$ 9,152	$ 22,657

Eat Your Way to Greater Wealth

I realize there have been several chapters dealing with food, but the reality is that for most American households, between eating at home and eating out, food can be a significant budget item.

An article in "Forbes" (April 30, 2012) referenced a Lehigh University study that found the extra medical costs of obese men average $1,152 a year, and of women, $3,613.

I realize celery or carrots are not nearly as tasty as potato chips and ice cream, so I'm not suggesting you give up all the "fun" food, but consider doing the "fun food" in moderation.

Maybe this story will help: Figuring I could live without sweets if I could indulge on the weekend, I went 5 full days with NO sugary stuff. Saturday morning I bought a dozen sweet, gooey, donuts. Nine donuts later .... I thought I was going to die. I was sick for 2 weeks. A valuable personal lesson in doing things in moderation.

Suppose we assume the average additional medical costs related to unhealthy eating habits averaged $2,000 a year, and because health care costs tend to increase we also assume the cost differential between a healthy lifestyle and one less so increased 5% a year.

The "Eat Your Way to Greater Wealth" table that follows shows the potential savings of a healthier lifestyle for just 10 years, but shows the wealth that could potentially result if that potential savings were left to grow for another 10 years.

You might find it interesting to calculate how much your investments could be worth in 20 years if you assumed the same7% rate of return and the annual savings increased 5% a year for the full 20 years. (Use Table FVA-5 in Appendix C with using the value where 20 years and 7% ROR intersect) Answer: $121,638

EAT YOUR WAY TO GREATER WEALTH

Cumulative			
Year	Savings	at 7%	7% MTE*
1	$2,000	$2,000	$140
2	$2,100	$4,240	$297
3	$2,205	$6,742	$472
4	$2,315	$9,529	$667
5	$2,431	$12,627	$884
....	$2,553	$16,063	$1,124
10	$3,103	$33,826	$2,368
.....		$36,193	$2,534
15		$47,442	$3,321
.....		$50,763	$3,553
20		$66,540	$4,658

* MTE = **M**oney **T**ree **E**ffect (see Chapter "What's an MTE?")

While it might be lots more fun to eat tasty but unhealthy foods – and as some friends tell me "I might not live that long," there could be some good reasons – such as several thousand dollars a year of extra income to enjoy in your later years – to help make the trade-off to a healthier lifestyle worth the effort and sacrifice.

F.A.N.A.F.I.

An often repeated point in "The Millionaire Mind" is that many of the deca-millionaires (worth $10 million or more) interviewed achieved success by seeing an opportunity others didn't see one, and used that opportunity to create a multi-million dollar business.

That is, they

....

Found

A

Need

And

Filled

It.

Some of the most successful entrepreneurs created a product (think *smartphone*) or service (think *Uber, Airbnb, Amazon,* or *Facebook*) for which no need existed, but millions of people can't imagine doing without today.

The reality is many of us just aren't "entrepreneur material." Particularly as we get older and see all the potential obstacles to success. It's a lot easier to stay in our comfort zone, get a check that provides a decent living, and go home at the end of the day without worrying whether there is enough money to meet the next payroll.

Years ago, a local businessman who at 16 started what became a hugely successful business making custom parts for Corvettes made the following comment during an interview:

"If I had known how difficult this was going to be, I never would have started."

In his book "The Cash Flow Quadrant," Robert "Rich Dad, Poor Dad": Kiyosaki postulates there are four basic means to earn income:

1. As an employee of someone else's business / organization
2. As a self-employed business in which the owner really IS the business and without whom the business would cease.
3. As a business owner with employees able to keep the business running and customers happy even if the owner is out of touch for long periods.
4. As an investor using a portion of ones savings to own shares of businesses that are operated by other people.

His main point: If you are an employee of a business, paid by the hour or a salary, or the owner of a business paid for services (think doctor or attorney), or products YOU make (think a florist, or surfboard shaper), your income is basically limited to the number of hours you could work and how much you could charge per hour.

As a business owner under his definition, even if you provide the same products or services (medical care, legal advice, floral arrangements, surfboards) as the self-employed person, if you have others doing the actual work, and a system or staff to run the business if you were not available, your potential income is not limited to the hours worked or charge per hour.

Finally, there is the investor. Through investments, the investor "employs" (has working) multiple businesses that can provide ongoing income (i.e.: dividends, gains from sale). Again, the investor's potential income is not limited to the hours he / she can work or what he / she might charge per hour.

While the potential of the business owner to create income and wealth is almost unlimited, for the investor, often wealth is limited by how much of their own income they can afford to invest, how well those investments do, and how well the investor manages those investments, but a key benefit of being an investor as the source of your wealth is that just about anyone with income can become a profitable investor.

Since statistics show that the majority of people who accumulate more than $5 million are business owners (including celebrities, athletes, etc. who ARE their business) or top executives, you might consider doing a SWOT analysis to identify your personal (S)trengths, (W)eaknesses, (O)pportunities and (T)hreats from the perspective of being the owner of "you as a business" rather than a salaried / hourly employee. Who knows what you might discover!

Consider the following story of a man in his 40's who had always had a JOB.

One day at a conference he got the idea to combine a badge clip with a lapel pin, and Clipeze were invented.

His first products were for employees of schools and hospitals because they all had to wear name badges, and the lanyard used to wear the badges kept getting in their way.

He was referred to me by mutual friends. He had been working second shift, so he had all day to do his Clipeze business. When his hours were changed to days he could no longer contact potential customers during normal business hours. Having worked at a JOB for over 20 years his focus was on being paid for his ***time***, not earning income based on "output." Our meeting provided a valuable lesson for both of us.

When I saw what he had created, it was obvious he had created something that "filled a need," and at an affordable price for his target market, which was huge.

After he told me the profit he made per item sold, and what he made at his job in a year, dividing the annual income by the item's profit, I calculated he needed to sell 55,000 of them to make what he earned in a year at his job. He looked at me with an "are you serious" look on his face and said "I could do that in two months if I could hit the major trade shows." To which I responded: "then it seems you have a choice of working two months or twelve months for the same amount of money."

My lesson came when he said "I've never thought about things that way," where pay wasn't related to hours worked, but to how many items needed to be sold to equal the income from his job.

Many people have a hobby they enjoy doing that when they lost their "job," were able to earn more money doing what they enjoyed, and many former employees who turned to freelance work to pay their bills found they could earn more working fewer hours being hired by multiple "employers" rather than just one.

What do you enjoy doing that you could earn enough to do that for a living?

Book Review

"The Top 10 Distinctions Between Millionaires and the Middle Class"

by Keith Cameron Smith

Some of the distinctions the author found include:

- People who remain of average wealth spend too much of their income on things that help others become millionaires.

- Millionaires play to win while others play to not lose.

- Millionaires believe they DESERVE to be successful.

- Millionaires have multiple sources of PASSIVE income – income generated by someone or something else.

- Millionaires believe acquiring knowledge to use for long-term improvement can be the greatest investment they make. They never stop trying to learn new things.

Look in your cupboard / pantry and closets. When you used YOUR money to buy THOSE things, who did it make richer?

Are there things others would pay you to do for them? This way THEIR money becomes YOUR money. Do you spend time learning new things that might help you become wealthier?

Obstacles versus Opportunities

- Saving too little vs. create ways to save more.
- Spending too much vs. create ways to spend less.
- Living too long vs. doing the above so that living longer is no longer an obstacle.

Squirrel-Proof Bird Feeder

I hadn't thought about the squirrels and my bird feeders in relation to financial independence until I listened to a book by Mark Sanborn titled "You Don't Need a Title to Be a Leader."

While the book doesn't have anything to do with financial planning or wealth accumulation, the story about him trying to find a squirrel-proof bird feeder had me laughing, as much from the story as from my own personal experience, and his comments about it got me thinking about its relevance to this book I was in the process of writing.

Shortly after I bought a home in "the country," Bobby and I put up a couple bird feeders on those curved-top poles. As with Mr. Sanborn, we probably spent over $100 trying different "squirrel-proof" bird feeders, only to have the squirrels figure out how to get to the birdseed in a matter of hours.

One funny aside before I share the lesson Mr. Sanborn shared: Since rain would not wash it away. One thing we did to try to keep the squirrels out of the bird feeders was to heavily grease the poles with Vaseline. We did get some good entertainment watching the squirrels launch themselves to grab about half-way up the pole, and then, slowly but surely, slide down as they struggled to hold on. But once they were able to "scrape off" the Vaseline, they were right back on the feeder eating away at the birdseed.

As Mr. Sanborn was complaining to the store owner where he bought this "squirrel-proof" bird feeder that it didn't stop the squirrels, but just took them a few more minutes to get their dinner, the store owner told him that the average person who buys a bird feeder may spend 15 minutes a day trying to think of ways to keep the squirrels at bay. But the squirrel spends 90% of its waking hours trying to figure out how to get to that bird-seed.

HIS CONCLUSION: "FOCUS AND DETERMINATION BEAT BRAINS AND INTELLECT ANY DAY OF THE YEAR"....in other words, without focus, it is virtually impossible to move forward to achieve your goals.

Bobby and I finally decided it was cheaper, and less time consuming, to just let the squirrels share what was in the feeder with the birds, and occasionally if we were near, use a hose to scare them off (*Note: We did think of using tar, but I didn't want to poison them, just get them to go elsewhere.*).

If we assume your goal, at least for reading this book, is to become financially independent by a certain age, and thus need to accumulate a DEFINED amount of PERSONAL wealth in a certain number of years (*assuming you will need more than social security, pension, inheritances, etc.*), then each CHOICE you make that increases your expenses, reduces your earnings, or reduces how much your investments earn, ultimately could be an obstacle to achieving your personal financial goals.

> ***Self-Sabotage***
> ***is often our greatest obstacle to any success.***
>
> ***90% of success is BELIEVING you have EARNED the right to reach your goal.***
>
> ***The key to achieving YOUR goals is to focus on the RIGHT thing.***

There Can Be "Gold" in Roomies

In the TV show "Golden Girls," four women live together in a house. The show's focus is the interaction between the women and the different perspectives they bring to their discussions, but from a financial perspective, it's also the story of women who gave up a little "independence" to afford to enjoy more of life.

With the advent of the "sharing society" and services such as *Airbnb*, *Uber*, and *ZipCar*, not having to own something on your own is becoming increasingly acceptable, but when someone graduates from college is divorced, or widowed, most want to live on their own. Sadly, for many the independence of living alone can result in being unable to afford to do many things they enjoy or be able to stop working and still afford an enjoyable lifestyle.

Consider this one example: My mom's apartment complex has a pool, exercise room, and walking trail, and the rental rates are:

- 1 bedroom / 1 bath for $735 / month
- 2 bedroom / 2 bath for $880 / month
- 3 bedroom / 3 bath for $960 / month

If we assume utilities are $100 / month for the 1 bedroom unit, and another $20 / month for each additional person, the cost would be $835 for the one bedroom, $1000 for the two bedroom, and $1100 for the three bedroom. If two people share the two bedroom, each would be paying $500 (saving $335/month), and if three people share the three bedroom, each would pay $367 (saving each $468 / month).

Suppose instead of living alone, for five years you and a friend shared a two bedroom apartment using the referenced rental rates. Based on savings of $335 a month ($4,020 a year) you would each be saving $20,100 in rent that could be used as a down payment on a new home, to pay off college debt, take a trip, etc. But what if you instead invested the savings earning 7% a year? The "Golden Girls" Approach to Wealth table illustrates how much those savings, could be worth in the years ahead.

A "GOLDEN GIRLS" APPROACH TO WEALTH

Year	On your own	Savings of 2 living together	Accumulated savings 7% ROR	2 living together 7% MTE
1	0	$4,020	$4,020	$281
2	0	$4,020	$8,321	$582
3	0	$4,020	$12,924	$905
4	0	$4,020	$17,849	$1,249
5	0	$4,020	$23,118	$1,618
::::				
10	0		$32,424	$2,270
::::::				
15	0		$45,477	$3,183
:::::				
20	0		$63,783	$4,465
:::::				
25	0		$89,459	$6,262
:::::				
30	0		$125,471	$8,783
INVESTED		$20,100		

ROR = Rate of return

MTE = **M**oney **T**ree **E**ffect (see Chapter "What's an MTE?")

Remember, this is not about sharing a house/apartment for 30 years, but about how much wealth / potential future income could result from having a roommate for just five years, and the extra income such a CHOICE could provide for splurges you might not otherwise afford.

Another option exists for someone who has become widowed or divorced and already has a house: rent out bedrooms (like in "Golden Girls") and invest all or part of the rent income.

A divorced client had a big house, with a big payment, that was impacting her ability to save for the future, so I suggested finding a roommate. Now obviously, you must be careful of who you have living in your home, but there are often people who would love to have the option of paying $300 or $400 for part of a nice house (and some companionship) versus the same or more living on their own.

Suppose my client charged $350 / month in rent, and utility costs increased $50 a month. That would be $300 a month ($3,600 / year) "extra" money she could invest.

The tables below show the "trade-off" of giving up some "privacy" in exchange for rent.

	No increase in rent		
Years	Amount invested	Invested at 7%	7% MTE
1	$3,600	$3,600	$252
2	$3,600	$7,452	$522
3	$3,600	$11,574	$810
4	$3,600	$15,984	$1,119
5	$3,600	$20,703	$1,449
.....			
10	$3,600	$49,739	$3,482
.....			
15	$3,600	$90,464	$6,332

3% / year increase in rent		
Amount invested	Invested at 7%	7% MTE
$3,600	$3,600	$252
$3,708	$7,560	$529
$3,819	$11,908	$834
$3,934	$16,676	$1,167
$4,052	$21,895	$1,533
$4,697	$56,091	$3,926
$5,445	$108,096	$7,567

ROR = Rate of return

MTE = **M**oney **T**ree **E**ffect (see Chapter "What's an MTE?")

Who's Afraid of the Big Bad Wolf?

For those not familiar with the story of the "Three Little Pigs." There are several versions, but basically, each of the pigs knew they needed to build a house to protect themselves from the big, bad wolf that wanted to eat them. The first pig built a house of straw, the second a house of twigs. Those houses went up quickly, so they spent the rest of the day singing and dancing.

The third little pig worked all day and built his house out of bricks. He didn't get to sing and play, but when the big, bad wolf came, the houses of the first two pigs were blown down. Fortunately for them, the third little pig let them come into his house, and it was strong enough that no matter how hard the wolf huffed and puffed, he could not blow the brick house down.

The idea of sound financial planning is to take the time to build a sound financial house of assets that can withstand the economic winds of taxes, inflation and unknowns.

Building a "financial house" follows the same concept as building a house. Each requires labor, material, tools and plans. The quality of these components is what ultimately determines the quality of the end product – be it a home, or a financial base.

Component One: MATERIAL. The material of the house may be wood, concrete, glass or a combination of different materials. The material of a "financial house" is money, or the investments / assets money can buy.

Component Two: LABOR. People and machines provide the labor in building a house. You earning income and SAVING a portion of what you earn, and your savings / money working (earning income) – are the workers building your future financial security.

Component Three: TOOLS. Hammers, saws, ladders, etc. are used to shape the basic materials to fit together so the whole is stronger than the parts. The tools of building an investment portfolio are the supermarket of investment options available to you as an investor.

Component Four: PLANS. The real key to success. Plans, assuming all the workers follow the plans, use the materials as specified, and use the tools as they were meant to be used, are designed (thought they don't always succeed) to ensure the desired house is the end product. Investment plans are developed to help an investor create an investment portfolio designed with the GOAL to create the future stream of income needed to finance a desired standard of living.

THE END RESULT: The main difference between the three houses of the little pigs was not the material. Even a house of straw – such as on many pacific islands – if properly constructed, can withstand strong winds. Rather, it is the tools used, the labor applied, and the plans – or lack thereof – that make the real difference.

The first two pigs wanted an instant solution so they could be done quickly and go out and play. They were not really concerned with anything except their immediate future. The third little pig spent time planning for the longer term. He knew about the wolf in the woods, and unlike his friends, wanted to be prepared for that danger. While he gave up a little fun in the meantime, had it not been for his planning and executing that plan to build a house that could keep out the wolf and other dangers to his safety, the wolf would have had a nice dinner and he would have lost his friends.

The primary difference is when it comes to your financial house, just because you assume a particular rate of return, investment, level of savings or inflation rate, doesn't mean it will happen. That makes it critically important that once you develop a plan, that you carefully and regularly monitor your progress.

A word of warning: financial planning doesn't work miracles. Its role is to help you find reasonable solutions to your financial concerns. Lots of money, or lots of compounding of money you invest, or lots of tools not used, will NOT a secure future make. PLANNING, and realizing that good things often take time, is generally the key to a secure home, and a portfolio of investments that can provide the income needed to have an enjoyable post work life.

You have the ability to get the "material," "labor," "tools," and "plans" for building a secure financial future. Money is only the "material." All the materials in the world will not make a house without labor and plans to construct it. You have some skill that will enable you to earn money (your material). Your financial house will not build itself. It is up to you to put your "material" to work in a way that increases your chances of having the financial house you desire, by the time you desire to "live" there.

Consider this story. Three high school friends – Strawman, Twigman, and Brickman.

Strawman goes to work for $20,000 a year and spends each evening "singing and dancing" with friends. Twigman and Brickman go to work with Strawman. Twigman also goes "singing and dancing" on weekends, but during the week he attends community college developing new skills. Brickman also spends his weekday evenings at school developing new skills, only going out every other weekend, and invests money he would have spent going out the other weekend in an IRA (assume it's 10% of income).

When Brickman and Twigman finish their AA degrees, they get a 20% raise (to $24,000 / year). Strawman is still earning $20,000.

Assuming those income levels continue for the next 40 years (*they'll all be 60 by then*), that Strawman saves nothing, Twigman saves 5% of his income starting in year three, and Brickman saves 10% from the start, here is what their finances would look like in the years ahead assuming their investments earned 7% a year:

Year	Strawman			Twigman			Brickman		
	Income	Savings	Wealth	Income	Savings	Wealth	Income	Savings	Wealth
1	$20,000	$0	$0	$20,000	$0	$0	$20,000	$2,000	$2,000
2	$20,000	$0	$0	$20,000	$0	$0	$20,000	$2,000	$4,140
3	$20,000	$0	$0	$24,000	$1,200	$1,200	$24,000	$2,400	$6,830
4	$20,000	$0	$0	$24,000	$1,200	$2,484	$24,000	$2,400	$9,708
5	$20,000	$0	$0	$24,000	$1,200	$3,858	$24,000	$2,400	$12,788
.....									
10	$20,000	$0	$0	$24,000	$1,200	$12,312	$24,000	$2,400	$31,737
.....									
15	$20,000	$0	$0	$24,000	$1,200	$24,169	$24,000	$2,400	$58,315
.....									
20	$20,000	$0	$0	$24,000	$1,200	$40,799	$24,000	$2,400	$95,591
...									
25	$20,000	$0	$0	$24,000	$1,200	$64,123	$24,000	$2,400	$147,873
.....									
30	$20,000	$0	$0	$24,000	$1,200	$96,837	$24,000	$2,400	$221,202
.....									
35	$20,000	$0	$0	$24,000	$1,200	$142,720	$24,000	$2,400	$324,049
.....									
40	$20,000	$0	$0	$24,000	$1,200	$207,073	$24,000	$2,400	$468,297

SUMMARY	Strawman	Twigman	Brickman
Total Income	$800,000	$952,000	$952,000
Total Savings	$0	$45,600	$95,200
40 year Wealth	$0	$207,073	$468,297
7% MTE*	$0	$14,495	$33,772

*MTE = **M**oney **T**ree **E**ffect see chapter "What's an MTE?"

All had the same potential. But they made different CHOICES, and in the end, Twigman and Brickman, while having more to spend than Strawman throughout those 40 years, each had more in savings than Strawman to generate extra income during the following years.

There's an old cliché that:
"What gets measured, gets done."
Maybe it does, maybe it doesn't,
but can it really hurt to keep a WRITTEN record
of your annual spending and saving
to chart your financial progress?

Will Inflation Steal Your Future?

If there were no such thing as inflation, it would be easy to calculate how much money you would need to provide for a lifetime of retirement income. All you would need to do is figure how much income you would need from investments each year, divide that by the rate of return you would earn, and the result would be how much money you needed to have to provide a fixed amount per year for as long as you would live. *(Income needed / rate of return = investment needed (I / R = P)*

For example, if there is no inflation, if the amount of income you needed each year to maintain your desired lifestyle stayed the same, for each $1,000 a year of income you needed from investments, assuming your investments earned 7%, you would need an investment of $14,285. ($1,000 / .07 = $14,285 ... proof: $14,285 x .07 = $1,000).

But life is seldom that simple. Odds are, even if your income is the same each year, the cost of food, electricity, clothing, and other things that make life enjoyable keep going up. Unless you are happy to buy less and less as you grow older, you will want enough money so your spendable income will at least keep up with YOUR personal cost of living.

Imagine, for example, that with the house paid for, kids grown and on their own, you were ready to stop working and have the financial freedom to live the life you've looked forward to enjoying, and you don't want to depend on social security, just in case the promised benefits aren't there. Understanding how inflation affects your income, and investment, needs could be critical to being able to maintain your standard of living should the cost of doing so keep increasing.

Since we don't really have any way of knowing EXACTLY what inflation will be, what rate of return your investments will earn, what taxes will be due, or.... HOW LONG YOU WILL LIVE ... the following table shows the amount of money you would need to have invested to be able to withdraw $30 a month (about $1 / day, $360 / year), for 25 years, assuming the investments earned 7%, and the cost of living increased 3% a year versus no increase per year.

For those not familiar with the terms used, the second column in each set (*investment needed at 7% / year*) shows the investment needed at the start of year 1 to generate the income for the future year indicated, and the third column of each set (*cumulative funding needed*) represents the total dollar amount, invested at 7%, to be able to withdraw the annual amount for the number of years indicated.

For example: referencing the first set of calculations, if you wanted to withdraw $360 a year for 10 years, you would need to invest $2,705 earning 7% to be able to withdraw that amount.

A LOOK AT INFLATION OVER TIME

Year	$30 / mo NO increase	Investment needed at 7% / year	Cumulative funding needed	$30 / mo 3% a yr increase	Investment needed at 7% / year	Cumulative funding needed
1	$360	$360		$360	$360	
2	$360	$336	$696	$371	$347	$707
3	$360	$314	$1,011	$382	$334	$1,040
4	$360	$294	$1,305	$393	$321	$1,361
5	$360	$275	$1,579	$405	$309	$1,670
::::						
10	$360	$196	$2,705	$470	$255	$3,051
::::						
15	$360	$140	$3,508	$545	$211	$4,192
:::::						
20	$360	$100	$4,081	$631	$175	$5,135
::::						
25	$360	$71	$4,489	$732	$144	$5,915

As you can see, referencing the second set of calculations, even with inflation of only 3%, the cost of living would more than double in 25 years (from $360 to $732).

Finally, for what it's worth, if you needed $3,000 a month at the start of retirement, instead of $30, you would need to multiply all the values in the table (other than the year) by 100. That means to generate $3,000 / month ($36,000 a year) for 10 years, you would need investments of $270,500 earning 7%, and if you wanted to increase your withdrawal by 3% a year, to be able to initially withdraw $3,000 / month ($36,000 / year) for 10 years, to generate that inflation adjusted income for 10 years you would need investments of $305,100 earning 7%. Both these calculations assume the principal (investment) is DEPLETED at the end of the stated time period.

The following table shows year by year, the income that would be withdrawn, and the investments remaining over the 10 year period if the same $36,000 were withdrawn each year.

YEAR BY YEAR DRAWDOWN OF $36,000 A YEAR

Initial Investment >>>		$270,500
Year	Withdrawal	End of year Remaining Balance
1	$36,000	$250,915
2	$36,000	$229,959
3	$36,000	$207,536
4	$36,000	$183,544
5	$36,000	$157,872
6	$36,000	$130,403
7	$36,000	$101,011
8	$36,000	$69,562
9	$36,000	$35,911
10	$36,000	($95)

As you can see, by the end of year 10, the $270,500 is essentially depleted ($95 shortfall due to rounding).

The following table shows the 10 year drawdown, but this time assuming withdrawals are increased 3% a year to seek to maintain an inflation adjusted income. Again, at the end of year 10, the initial investment is almost completed depleted ($3.00 left due to rounding).

YEAR BY YEAR DRAWDOWN ADJUSTED FOR 3% A YEAR INCREASE

Initial Investment >>>		$305,100
Year	Withdrawal	End of year Remaining Balance
1	$36,000	$287,937
2	$37,080	$268,417
3	$38,192	$246,340
4	$39,338	$221,492
5	$40,518	$193,642
6	$41,734	$162,542
7	$42,986	$127,925
8	$44,275	$89,505
9	$45,604	$46,974
10	$46,972	$3

While it is always possible that inflation will disappear for the years you are retired, it's not something I would suggest counting on when you "do the math" to figure out how much you would need to finance your desired post-work lifestyle.

Time Can Be Your Friend, or Foe

And the choice is YOURS! But the longer you wait, the harder it likely will be to accumulate the wealth necessary to finance your desired lifestyle, because in the process of accumulating wealth, time may be your greatest ally, or enemy.

Take this simple example. Suppose you invested money and it earned 7% a year. The Getting to a Million table shows the initial investment needed (*rounded to the nearest dollar*), to accumulate $1 million in the number of years indicated, with the second column assuming the annual investment remains the same each year, and the third column assuming the initial investment as shown, but the annual amount invested each year would increase 3% / year.

GETTING TO A MILLION

Years to reach goal	Annual investment fixed amount / year	Initial investment increasing 3% / year
45	$3,500	$2,323
40	$5,010	$3,416
35	$7,234	$5,088
30	$10,587	$7,716
25	$15,812	$11,999
20	$24,393	$19,384
15	$39,795	$33,304
10	$72,380	$64,185

As you can see, for someone who has 45 years to reach that goal of $1 million, or even 40 years, the investment needed is fairly reasonable – an amount someone could earn working extra hours, or cutting expenses by $10 - $15 / day. But once you have 25 years or less for your investments to accumulate, the investment amount needed has gone up dramatically, and for too many, earning that much more, or cutting expenses that much, could be quite difficult.

And it's not just time that can be an enemy. It can be a lack of perspective. For example, how do you actually define "savings"?

In a recent article, a young woman being interviewed was asked the best business advice she had received. She said "work hard, don't live beyond your means, and be diligent about saving your money." That sounds great. But then she went on to say those were words of wisdom that led her to being able to buy a BRAND-NEW CAR by the age of 21. If her goal was to build wealth so she could one day stop working, could she honestly say she was diligent about SAVING her money?

Now, suppose instead of a new car, she purchased a used car and net of maintenance costs, she saved the equivalent of $1,000 / year for six years. If we assume she bought this used car at 21, and the savings from buying a used car earned 7% a year, at the end of six years (when she would be 27). She would have saved $7,153. That money, created from the savings of buying a used car that ONE time, invested for another 35 years (to age 62) would have created "TRUE SAVINGS (i.e.: WEALTH)" of $76,373.

Again, THE CHOICE IS YOURS... Each dollar you spend today is money no longer available to work for your tomorrow, but if you invest those dollars wisely, and leave them to work for you during your working years, you might just accumulate enough dollars working for you that you no longer have to work for them.

Book Review

"START WHERE YOU ARE"

by Chris Gardner

A key factor of getting where you want to go is knowing where you ARE when you start.

The book and movie "The Pursuit of Happyness" is about Chris Gardner's journey from living in a car to becoming a successful financial advisor and motivational speaker.

The focus throughout his book, much like mine, is that life, at its core, is about CHOICES, and a key point he makes is that the past - is passed. It is gone. You can learn from it, but if you dwell on what went wrong, or how life has not been fair, or believe it's someone else's fault "you are where you are," then you make it virtually impossible to change your future for the better.

One story that really stuck in my mind was about a woman who introduced herself to him at one of his presentation. She told him about growing up in a bad neighborhood where walking to school she was constantly tempted to go another way, but she stuck to her goal of getting an education and having a career and a life she was proud to provide her children and serve as their role model.

In the book, Mr. Gardner offers five words he feels are the basis for someone to turn their dreams (goals) into reality:

CLEAR
CONCISE
COMPELLING
COMMITTED
CONSISTENT

In a nutshell, he advises when you have a goal you want to achieve:

- It must be CLEAR. You must be able to clearly picture that goal (for example, your desired lifestyle) in your mind.

- It must be CONCISE. You should be able to describe that goal (for example, the amount of money you need to afford that lifestyle) in a few words.

- It must be COMPELLING. It must be something you want so passionately that you are willing, without harming or misusing others, to change your lifestyle, even your friends if needed, to reach your goal, to fulfill your dream.

Once you have clearly and concisely stated your goal (in writing), and defined for yourself your compelling reason to want to achieve it, then it is up to you to:

- COMMIT to doing what needs to be done (legally and ethically) to make this goal a reality, and

- Take positive action to CONSISTENTLY do what needs to be done to make your goal a reality.

Needless to say, there is no guarantee that even if you do all these things you will reach your desired goal. Life isn't always fair, but by aligning your daily thoughts and activities with your goal, by creating a true plan to get where you want to go, your odds of succeeding are greatly increased.

What does the future hold? *Only time will tell. But by tracking your spending and saving - having an actual "spending plan" that you don't just create, but use to compare against actual spending and saving - and taking control of your finances instead of them controlling you, when opportunities come your way, you could be better prepared to take advantage of those opportunities, particularly those requiring a financial investment.*

Leisure Time Income

An article in the New York Daily News on 3/5/14 referenced a Nielsen study stating the average American watches TV, or sits at a computer playing games or "Facebooking" thirty-five hours a week. Time that could be put to productive (i.e.: income producing) use.

Suppose spending one evening a week preparing lunch for the following week saved you $30 each week. That would be $1,500 a year. Or suppose you got a part-time job one night a week (50 weeks a year) and earned $30 a week net of taxes and expenses. That again would be $1,500 a year of potential "wealth" income.

And it doesn't have to be "forever." Suppose for 5 years you earned or saved $30 a week in place of watching TV or playing on the computer and invested that earnings / savings.

LEISURE TIME WEALTH

Year	Invested	Accumulated at 7%	7% MTE*
1	$1,500	$1,500	$105
2	$1,500	$3,105	$217
3	$1,500	$4,822	$338
4	$1,500	$6,660	$466
5	$1,500	$8,626	$604
.....			
10		$12,099	$847
.....			
20		$23,800	$1,666
.....			
30		$46,818	$3,277

*MTE = **M**oney **T**ree **E**ffect (see Chapter "What's an MTE?")

Even if you only reinvested the savings for 20 years, that's still potential "lifetime" income of over $100 a month to do what you want, when you want - in exchange for trading four-five hours a week, for just five years, doing something that could add fuel to your "personal wealth machine" instead of watching TV.

Little Things Can Matter

If you have ever tried to lose weight, you know how important it is to keep a record of everything you eat.

I've had to watch my weight since I was 18. A couple years ago I hit my highest weight ever and decide it was time for professional help.

The first week, I ate more than I had been eating before, but I lost 6 pounds, and 2 inches in my hips, and shoulders. Within 2 months, I had only lost about 13 pounds, but by eating right, I had gone down 2 pant sizes. The key was weighing all I ate, recording it in my "food log," and having to be accountable to a counselor.

I believe applying a similar concept to money - the consistent tracking of what you are spending, and investing - can be a key ingredient in accumulating wealth.

To see how small things can matter, consider this story about a woman who at age 45 weighed 400 pounds. 25 years earlier, at age 20, she had weighed just 125 pounds. A gain of 275 pounds in 25 years.

As I've told this story through the years, I asked each person to guess how many extra calories a day (on average) this woman had eaten to gain 275 pounds in 25 years. The estimates ranged from 300 to 1,500 calories a day. Here were the calculations I showed them:

- 3,500 calories per pound (according to my brother the doctor)
- 275 pounds gained
- 3,500 calories / pound x 275 pounds = 962,500 extra calories consumed
- 365 days per year (leap year days ignored)
- 25 years
- 365 days / year * 25 years = 9,125 total days in 25 years

Which means this woman had eaten 962,500 extra calories in 9,125 days.

Result: 962,500 extra calories eaten in 9,125 days. Divide 962,500 calories by 9,125 days you get .... **105**. That's all the extra calories a day she ate!

That's the difference between a hamburger and a cheeseburger, plain toast versus buttered, a cup of carrots or celery versus 12 regular potato chips.

On the TV show "The Biggest Loser," a key part of the program was not just exercise, but learning to eat correctly.

I know, their only job was to lose weight and they had daily coaching as well. And yes, some contestants gained back the weight they lost, but many not only maintained their weight loss, but helped others do the same.

I particularly liked the weigh-in's being based on a percentage, so if Sue weighs less than Joe, even if she lost fewer pounds, if the percentage of her original weight lost was higher she still won. It's the same with investing. Actual dollars earned on an investment are based on the dollars invested and the rate of return earned.

Just as eating 105 fewer calories than you burn a day can result in almost a pound of weight lost in a month, even a small change in the rate of return your investments earn, or the percent by which you increase your annual investment amount, or saving an extra hundred or two dollars a month affects the wealth you might accumulate.

There are phone apps to track spending, but I personally encourage clients who truly want to become wealthy to start by carrying a 3"x5" spiral notebook, and as soon as they spend money, whether cash, check or credit card, to write down all spending.

Being "penny wise" could start you on the path to increased prosperity.

LITTLE THINGS, DONE REGULARLY, CAN ADD UP.
And when it comes to money being invested, you have the added power of compounding.

What a Difference a Year Makes

Many clients are surprised at the difference a year can make when it comes to wealth accumulation. The table below shows the "cost of waiting" if investing $1,000 a year starting at 21, 22, and 26 assuming the money invested earns 7% a year.

Year-end value from investing $1000 a year earning 7%

Age	Start at age 21	Start at age 22	Start at age 26
21	$1,000		
22	$2,070	$1,000	
23	$3,215	$2,070	
24	$4,440	$3,215	
25	$5,751	$4,440	
26	$7,153	$5,751	$1,000
27	$8,654	$7,153	$2,070
28	$10,260	$8,654	$3,215
29	$11,978	$10,260	$4,440
30	$13,816	$11,978	$5,751
.....			
40	$40,995	$37,379	$25,129
.....			
50	$94,459	$87,347	$63,248
.....			
60	$199,631	$185,641	$138,234
.....			
65	$285,744	$266,122	$199,631

Of course, the 21 year old invested a total of $45,000 while the 22 year only invested $44,000, and the 26 year old invested only

$40,000, but at age 65 the 21-year-old investor's $45,000 was worth $19,622 more than the investor who started a year later, and $86,113 more than the investor who didn't start until 5 years later. Some might say that's not a bad "trade for wealth."

Now take the above table one step further and compare the **M**oney **T**ree **E**ffect (MTE) of starting at 21, versus 26.

5 YEAR DIFFERENCE MONEY TREE EFFECT

Age	Start at age 21	Age 21 7% MTE	Start at age 26	Age 26 7% MTE	7% MTE difference
21	$1,000	$70			$70
22	$2,070	$145			$145
23	$3,215	$225			$225
24	$4,440	$311			$311
25	$5,751	$403			$403
26	$7,153	$501	$1,000	$70	$431
27	$8,654	$606	$2,070	$145	$461
28	$10,260	$718	$3,215	$225	$493
29	$11,978	$838	$4,440	$311	$528
30	$13,816	$967	$5,751	$403	$565
::::					
40	$40,995	$2,870	$25,129	$1,759	$1,111
:::					
50	$94,459	$6,612	$63,248	$4,427	$2,185
:::					
60	$199,631	$13,974	$138,234	$9,676	$4,298
:::					
65	$285,744	$20,002	$199,631	$13,974	$6,028

By the time each is 65, the extra $5,000 the 21 year old had invested would allow him to withdraw over $6,000 a year more than the investor who started at 26, "forever." If they both lived another 25 years (to age 90), that would be more than $150,000 of extra income in exchange for starting a modest investment program five years sooner.

Procrastination can be one of the greatest obstacles in a quest for financial independence.

Credit Your Score

The purpose of this chapter is to help someone with a lower credit score decide if it could make sense to improve their credit score before buying a house and rent in the interim. NOTE: If you anticipate prices to rise quickly and substantially, even if you are paying a higher rate you may be better off buying now, and refinancing later if it makes financial sense.

The following information is from www.myfico.com as of 3/18/2016 the highest and lowest FICO scores for a 30-year mortgage.

30 YEAR MORTGAGE - $100,000

FICO SCORE	Rate	Monthly	Total Interest
760 - 850	3.354%	$441	$58,736
620 - 639	4.943%	$533	$92,004

While many home buyers focus on the total interest they would be paying, from a "wealthy choices" perspective, a better way to compare mortgages might be as a business would compare two different projects to decide which was most profitable.

The calculation used for this analysis is known as the *Net Present Value* of an annuity. The value calculated represents the amount of money each borrower would need to invest up front at the assumed investment return to be able to withdraw the annual mortgage payment each year until the mortgage was paid off.

The tables to use are in Appendix D. Since it is assumed the mortgage is a fixed amount per year, use Table PVA-0 from Appendix D.

Since the mortgage being considered is a 30-year mortgage, you would use the 30 year column. The assumed rate of return (ROR) –

technically known as the "discount rate" for this type of calculation - to use is the rate you feel you could realistically earn on an investment assuming a 30-year investment period. For this example, assume a discount rate of 5%.

Based on the assumptions of a 30-year time period and 5% assumed investment return, the multiplier would be the value ($16,141) where the 30 year column / 5% row intersect.

The payment for the borrower with the lower credit score is $533 a month, or $6,396 per year. Since the table is based on an initial $1,000, you would divide $6,396 by $1,000 = 6.396. 6.396 multiplied by the 30 year / 5% factor of $16,141 = $103,238.

The payment for the borrower with the higher credit score is $441 a month, or $5,292 per year. Again, since the table is based on an initial $1,000, you would divide $5,292 by $1,000 = 5.292. 5.292 multiplied by the 30 year/5% factor of $16,141 = $85,418.

The difference is $17,820. That means the person with the lower credit score would need to invest $17,820 more to make payments for the life of the mortgage on the $100,000 initially assumed to be borrowed.

Anything is Possible if You Believe

Wouldn't that be a wonderful "mantra" for your life!

When interviewed after finally completing the 110-mile swim from Miami to Cuba at age 64, Diana Nyad said one should not be afraid of failing – that they should use each failure as a lesson to grow from, and that her mantra through life had been to "Find a Way" (which is also the title of her book).

Too often, when a person fails at something, they see themselves as a failure. But unless what was involved was a life or death situation, they really created a "Learning Opportunity." The question is whether they will focus on the failure, or what they can learn from it to do better next time.

A romance novel I read many years ago, had this great line:

"You can't turn back the clock,
but you can wind it up again."

If you find yourself focusing on what you did wrong, or what didn't go right, consider the following quotes from Thomas Edison, one of the greatest inventors of all time who had (individually or jointly) been granted more than 1,000 patents.

"I have not failed.
I've just found 10,000 ways that won't work."

"Many of life's failures are people who did not realize how close they were to success when they gave up."

"Our greatest weakness lies in giving up. The most certain way to succeed is always to try just one more time."

The reality is that investing, whether in your own business or in businesses started and run by others, has risks. It is virtually GUARANTEED at some point in time your investments will be worth less than you have invested. In fact, it is likely to happen more than once if you invest for the long term.

But NOT investing, depending on what others promise but may not deliver, could leave you in a far worse financial position than losing money occasionally in your investment portfolio.

The key is to understand what you are investing in. What risks are likely, versus what potential rewards might result. And to not consider losing money as a personal failure, but a natural part of building a portfolio to provide the income you may need in your later years.

> ***"Seeing yourself as being worthy of being wealthy is the first step to achieving it."*** – Ilene Davis

Millionaire in the Making Support Group

One the most difficult things for many people to do is to say "no" to friends.

If your goal is to become wealthy, but you hang out with spenders, you are more likely to spend along with them. You might find it is more fun, and less stressful, to find others who also want to become millionaires, start a "Millionaire in the Making Support Group" (you'll need to create your own "step" program) and create your own "low cost" entertainment program of fun things to do that don't cost a lot of money (maybe even use some of the ideas in this book).

For example, couldn't you have as much fun eating, drinking and working together on a giant jigsaw puzzle for an evening as going out where the music is so loud you can barely hear yourself think, much less hear the person next to you? Or maybe even generate some profit from having fun by creating events that are fun and others will pay to attend.

6 MONTH REVIEW

1. Outside of regular monthly or quarterly bills, make a list of everything you spent in the past six months and what you spent it on. Break this list into categories: food, clothing, eating out, entertainment, etc. Once you have that done, see what you remember about those purchases, and if you really feel that was money well spent. If not, try this next:

2. Moving forward, each time you go to buy something, ask yourself a simple question: "If I don't buy this today, six months from now, will I really regret it, or even remember?" If not, put the money you would have spent, IN CASH, in a jar. Once every three months,

take the money out, count it, take 10% to buy yourself a "reward" and put the rest in your "millionaire fund." REPEAT – preferably on an ongoing basis.

Odds are, you will find you can have just as much fun in life, and a lot more wealth, by only buying what you really believe you will remember just six months later.

And if you have a group that support each other in doing this, with members sharing not just fun events, but hopefully sharing ideas with each other about ways members have found to save money, alerting others about special sales, or even get together to do a "group buy" of items you can all use that you might be able to buy for less in larger quantity at a wholesale type store and then pay your individual share.

There are hundreds of ways to enjoy life while saving money. Since each person has different reasons why the savings "aren't worth it," I challenge you to think of five things for which you could find an equally viable but less expensive substitute / alternative.

Retirement Nest Egg Starter Kit

Back in 1982, when I started as a financial advisor, my focus was to get as many people as I could saving SOMETHING for their future.

I came up with this little ditty that not only was short and simple, but even rhymed:

"A dollar or two a day,
saved instead of spent,
could add some extra income
to your retirement

I even created a "Retirement Nest Egg Starter Kit" (see below and referenced in the story about the young father in the chapter titled "J. Paul Getty is a Billionaire). The only change in the past 30 years is the daily recommended savings has been increased to $5 a day to adjust for inflation.

When someone says, "they may NEED that money," I point out that's one reason I recommend a plastic soda bottle. They can see their money "growing," if they truly need it they can cut the bottle open, but as they cut, they'll at least have a few minutes to think about whether this is the smart CHOICE to make.

If you are struggling to get started on the path to wealth, think about this single father with four children to support, and consider giving the following idea a try:

RETIREMENT NEST EGG STARTER KIT

1. Get (or create) an empty 2-liter soda bottle.

2. Make a copy of the following label.

3. Tape the label on the empty soda bottle.
4. Put it in a safe but convenient place.
5. Follow the instructions on the label each day.

RETIREMENT NEST EGG STARTER KIT

1. Roll up a $5.00 bill (*or at least a dollar or two if that's all you can do on some days*)
2. As you insert it into the soda bottle, repeat (preferably out loud) "Five or ten dollars a day, saved instead of spent, could increase my income during retirement"
3. Mark off the next number on the chart below
4. Repeat 1 through 3 until the last number is crossed off

1	**2**	**3**	**4**	**5**	**6**	**7**	**8**	**9**	**10**
11	**12**	**13**	**14**	**15**	**16**	**17**	**18**	**19**	**20**
21	**22**	**23**	**24**	**25**	**26**	**27**	**28**	**29**	**30**
31	**32**	**33**	**34**	**35**	**36**	**37**	**38**	**39**	**40**
41	**42**	**43**	**44**	**45**	**46**	**47**	**48**	**49**	**50**
51	**52**	**53**	**54**	**55**	**56**	**57**	**58**	**59**	**60**

If you invest the $5 each day for 60 days, you will have $300. If you put $100 in savings, set up a $100 / month systematic investment plan into an investment fund, you'll still have$100 to set aside for the next month. If you continue to invest $5 / day, you would be adding $100 / month to your retirement plan, and $50 a month to your savings.

It's YOUR CHOICE. But a couple dollars a day that likely won't be missed could add up to big bucks over the years ahead.

Three Questions

Yes, these are the same questions in the chapter titled "Financial Intelligence," and while there may be no actual link to the wealth accumulated by those who answered all the questions correctly and those who answered none correctly, my personal conclusion is if someone doesn't understand how money can compound over time, particularly when they have 20-30 years to invest, they have little incentive to give up the enjoyment that can come from spending money today if they don't understand how even small investments, left to grow for years, can increase substantially in value.

I personally believe understanding these concepts is a key factor in helping you make "wealthy choices," so I'm including them again. (*Plus, if you didn't read that chapter, you'll have a chance to try to answer the questions for the first time.*)

As mentioned before, the questions were included in a 2006 paper co-authored by Professors Annamaria Lusardi and Olivia S. Mitchell titled "Financial Literacy and Planning: Implications for Retirement Wellbeing." (*Lusardi, Annamaria and Olivia S. Mitchell (2015). "Financial Literacy and Economic Outcomes: Evidence and Policy Implications. Journal of Retirement Economics. 3(1): 107-114. Available at http://www.pensionresearchcouncil.org/publications/pdf/JEL_FinLit_LusardiMitchell2-12-14.pdf)*

To repeat, the three questions were:

1. Suppose you had $100 in a savings account and the interest rate was 2% per year. After five years, how much would you have in the account if you left the money to grow: more than $102, exactly $102, less than $102?

2. Imagine that the interest rate on your savings account was 1% per year and inflation was 2% per year. After 1 year, would you be able to buy more than, exactly the same as, or less than what you could buy today with the money in this account?

3. Do you think that the following statement is true or false? "Buying a single company stock usually provides a safer return than a stock mutual fund."

If you couldn't answer these questions before, you are not alone.

According to the referenced paper, 67.1% correctly answered question 1 correctly, 75.2% answered question 2 correctly, and 52.3% answered question 3 correctly.

Only 34.3% of the couples answered all three questions correctly.

And remember what Arkad (mentioned in the chapter titled "Arkad's Lesson") told his friends is at the heart of the accumulation of wealth.

"The reason most people fail to achieve more than a bare existence is because they have either failed to learn the rules for building wealth, or have failed to observe them."

What you don't know CAN hurt you.

By the way, the answers to the 3 questions:

1. More than $102

2. You would be able to buy less

3. False

How did you do?

Will You Take the Vow?

Anyone can accumulate wealth if they CHOOSE to do so. But it can help to make a commitment, if only to yourself.

FINANCIAL FITNESS VOW

I, ______________________________, would like to have sufficient financial resources by the age of _____, to be free to quit working and still be able to afford the lifestyle I have envisioned for myself (and my family).

It would cost me $_______________ a year to have such a lifestyle today.

I understand achieving this goal will take time, effort and discipline on my part.

I understand I will need to learn to set my priorities, invest regularly, and manage my investments wisely.

I believe the rewards of these efforts will be worth the tasks required of me.

I pledge to myself, and my loved ones, to make every effort to succeed at this goal.

Signed ____

Date _______________

It's YOUR future.
Your choices between now and "then" could define what your future becomes.

A Sample Calculation

Meet Joe: He is currently 45 and wants to retire in 20 years. The lifestyle he hopes to have will cost $40,000 in current dollars. He expects the average cost of living for his desired lifestyle to increase 3% a year, and assumes after taxes, his investments will earn an average 6% between now and his desired retirement, and 4% a year during his post work years. Finally, he expects to live 30 years after he retires.

For planning purposes, he is assuming no income from social security or a pension. Calculating how much in personal assets he will need at the start of retirement is a two-step process.

1. Based on his projected retirement income needs in current dollars, calculate the inflation adjusted income he would need 20 years from now.

2. Based on the future income needed calculated in Step 1, calculate how much he would need to finance his desired level of spending through his projected 30 years of retirement.

This particular calculation, because of the way the tables in the Appendix A are structured, it a little more complex than doing just a single calculation.

STEP 1: CALCULATING "FIRST YEAR OF RETIREMENT" INCOME NEEDED

Table FVS-1 calculates the end of year value of a beginning of the year investment, so for someone who will retire 20 years from now, the first year of retirement is assumed to be year 21.

Using Table FVS-1 from Appendix A, you will see the value at the intersection of 3% ROR and year 20 is $1,806.

Because Table FVS-1 assumes an initial amount of $1,000, Joe would need to divide his assumed $40,000 of current income by $1,000 to get the proper "cost of living multiplier." In this case, the value would be $40,000 divided by $1,000 = 40.

To calculate the year 21 inflation adjusted equivalent of $40,000, Joe would multiply the 20-year value from Table FVS-1 ($1,806) by 40 = $72,240. That means at the start of year 21, which would be the first year of his retirement, based on the assumptions used, Joe would need income of $72,240 to have the same inflation adjusted purchasing power as he has with $40,000 today.

STEP 2: CALCULATING RETIREMENT FUNDING NEEDED

Once Joe has calculated his first-year retirement income needs, he would calculate the total funding required to finance his desired retirement lifestyle. (NOTE: I recommend adding five years to the life expectancy you assume- *"Better to have money left at the end of life than life at the end of the money.")*

Joe has made the following assumptions regarding his retirement years:

- 3% a year increase in his cost of living.
- 30 years life expectancy.
- 4% net earnings on his investments.

(NOTE: Because social security and pensions benefit will depend on when they would start, and your age when you begin receiving them, if you are including them in your funding needs calculation, you will need to calculate their "retirement value" as well.)

The initial amount calculated in Step 1($72,240) would be divided by 1,000, so Joe's multiplier would be $72.24. Joe expects to live for 30 years, and expects his investments to earn 4% per year net of taxes.

Joe's cost of living increase is assumed to be 3% a year. Appendix D provides four different tables to use to calculate the investment needed to withdraw / generate a specified level of income for a specified number of years into the future. In this case, the relevant table (PVA-3) provides values when the annual withdrawal increase per year (AWIPY) is assumed to be 3%.

Since Joe is assuming a 4% per year investment return and 30-year withdrawal period, the "investment needed multiplier" Joe would use is $26,169.

That means to calculate the amount of investment he needs to finance his desired lifestyle, Joe would multiply the "income needed multiplier" ($72.24) by the "investment needed multiplier" ($26,169). The result: $1,890,448.

Since these calculations are often not taught in school, I've provided a year by year table titled "Meet Joe" showing a 3% increase in the cost of living starting at $40,000 in year 1. Calculations for both Step 1 and Step 2 are provided.

The table shows the annual cost of living for the first year of retirement is $72,244 (using the tables, the value calculated is $72,240 - a $4 difference due to rounding error).

In the top box of the table, you will see the value ($1,890,448) calculated in Step 2.

The last column on the "Meet Joe" table shows the balance of the "funding amount" remaining at the end of each year. You will see a shortfall of $493 in the 30th year of the "remaining balance" column. This again is due to values in Tables FVS-1 and PVA-3 being rounded to even dollar amounts. Still, an error of only $493 out of almost $2 million suggests the accuracy of the tables in the Appendix for general planning purposes.

For many readers, this calculation can be quite intimidating, but the more you work out these calculations with some different assumptions, the more comfortable you hopefully will become in using them.

Retirement Funds Needed* >>>$1,890,448						
Year	Joe's age	Desired income	Year of retirement	Joes age	Income needed	Remaining balance
1	45	$40,000	1	65	$72,244	$1,890,932
2	46	$41,200	2	66	$74,412	$1,889,181
3	47	$42,436	3	67	$76,644	$1,885,038
4	48	$43,709	4	68	$78,943	$1,878,338
5	49	$45,020	5	69	$81,312	$1,868,908
6	50	$46,371	6	70	$83,751	$1,856,563
7	51	$47,762	7	71	$86,264	$1,841,111
8	52	$49,195	8	72	$88,852	$1,822,350
9	53	$50,671	9	73	$91,517	$1,800,066
10	54	$52,191	10	74	$94,263	$1,774,036
11	55	$53,757	11	75	$97,090	$1,744,023
12	56	$55,369	12	76	$100,003	$1,709,781
13	57	$57,030	13	77	$103,003	$1,671,048
14	58	$58,741	14	78	$106,093	$1,627,553
15	59	$60,504	15	79	$109,276	$1,579,008
16	60	$62,319	16	80	$112,554	$1,525,112
17	61	$64,188	17	81	$115,931	$1,465,548
18	62	$66,114	18	82	$119,409	$1,399,984
19	63	$68,097	19	83	$122,991	$1,328,073
20	64	$70,140	20	84	$126,681	$1,249,447
21	65	$72,244	21	85	$130,482	$1,163,724
			22	86	$134,396	$1,070,501
			23	87	$138,428	$969,357
			24	88	$142,581	$859,847
			25	89	$146,858	$741,508
			26	90	$151,264	$613,854
			27	91	$155,802	$476,375
			28	92	$160,476	$328,535
			29	93	$165,290	$169,775
			30	94	$170,249	–$493

*calculated using the tables in the Appendix

How to Use the Tables in the Appendix

Most of the examples used in the book assumed any money invested earned 7% a year, whether it was reinvested or taken as MTE (**M**oney **T**ree **E**ffect) income.

But different investors have different risk tolerances and investment experience and not all may be comfortable with a large portion of their savings invested in stocks.

The tables in each Appendix provide calculation information for investment returns of 0% to 8%. In addition, for calculations that involve multiple years of income or investment, tables are provided that allow you to assume annual increases of 1%, 3% and 5%, as well as a fixed rate (0%).

Often the biggest challenge is knowing what table needs to be used in solving a particular type of financial scenario.

Each Appendix has a more detailed explanation; however, a quick overview might be useful.

If you want to know what something is likely to cost, or be worth in the future, you would use Appendix A.

If you are expecting to receive a lump sum in the future and want to know what it would be worth in current dollars you would use Appendix B.

If you are planning to make annual investments and want to know what their total value would be at some time in the future, you would use Appendix C.

If you want to know how much you would need to invest to be able to make annual withdrawals for a specified period of time, you would use Appendix D. This Appendix can also be used if you expect a future stream of income (such as a pension) and want to know how much you would need to invest as a lump sum to equal that amount.

If you know you have a certain amount of funds and want to know how much you could afford to draw out in year one so your funds would last a specified number of years, you would use Appendix E.

If you are seeking to accumulate a specified future amount by making investments over two or more years, and want to know how much you would need to invest the first year, you would use Appendix F.

Notes

Appendix A:

FUTURE VALUE / COST OF SINGLE AMOUNT

NOTE: Values provided are based on an initial amount of $1,000.

FVS-1 assumes the investment is made at the start of year 1 and the value computed is for the end of the indicated year.

WHEN TO USE FVS-1: When you want to know what a specified amount of money, invested at a specified annual rate of return, would be worth at a specified number of years in the future. For example, you currently have $20,000 in investments and want to know what it would be worth in 30 years if it earned 4% a year.

HOW TO USE FVS-1: Once you choose the number of years (column) the funds would be invested, and the rate of return (row) assumed to be earned, find the value where the column / row intersect. This is your "future value multiplier." Since the values in the table are based on an initial investment of $1,000, divide the actual investment amount by $1,000 to calculate the "investment multiplier." Multiply the "future value multiplier" by the "investment multiplier" to calculate the future value of your actual investment.

TEST YOURSELF USING FVS-1: Assume an investment of $85,000, a rate of return of 6%, and you want to know what that investment would be worth in 20 years. (Answer: $272,595)

FVS–1: Future value of a $1,000 investment

TABLE FVS-1									
	YEARS IN FUTURE AMOUNT IS CALCULATED								
ROR*	5	10	15	20	25	30	40	50	60
0%	$1,000	$1,000	$1,000	$1,000	$1,000	$1,000	$1,000	$1,000	$1,000
1	$1,051	$1,105	$1,161	$1,220	$1,282	$1,348	$1,489	$1,645	$1,817
2	$1,104	$1,219	$1,346	$1,486	$1,640	$1,811	$2,208	$2,692	$3,281
3	$1,159	$1,344	$1,558	$1,806	$2,094	$2,427	$3,262	$4,384	$5,892
4	$1,217	$1,480	$1,801	$2,191	$2,666	$3,243	$4,801	$7,107	$10,520
5	$1,276	$1,629	$2,079	$2,653	$3,386	$4,322	$7,040	$11,467	$18,679
6	$1,338	$1,791	$2,397	$3,207	$4,292	$5,743	$10,286	$18,420	$32,988
7	$1,403	$1,967	$2,759	$3,870	$5,427	$7,612	$14,974	$29,457	$57,946
8	$1,469	$2,159	$3,172	$4,661	$6,848	$10,063	$21,725	$46,901	$101,257

*ROR = Rate of return

FVS–2 assumes the amount is the year 1 cost and calculates the value for the year in the future indicated.

WHEN TO USE FVS-2: When you want to know how much something would cost a specific number of years in the future adjusted for projected inflation / increase in the cost of living. For example, you want to know how much income you would need in 10 years to have the same purchasing power as $30,000 in current dollars if the cost of living increased an average 3% a year between now and then.

HOW TO USE FVS-2: Once you choose the number of years (column) into the future for which to calculate and the average inflation rate (row) during those years, find the value where the column / row intersect. This is your "future cost multiplier." Since the values in the table are based on an initial cost of $1,000, divide the actual current annual cost by $1,000 to calculate the "current cost multiplier." Multiply the "future cost multiplier" by the "current cost multiplier" to calculate the inflation adjusted future cost of your specified current lifestyle.

TEST YOURSELF USING FVS-2: Assume your desired future lifestyle costs $50,000 in current dollars, inflation averages 3%, and you want to know the annual cost of that equivalent lifestyle in 25 years. (Answer: $101,650)

FVS–2: Future inflation-adjusted cost of initial $1,000 a Year

TABLE FVS-2									
YEARS IN FUTURE COST OF LIVING IS CALCULATED									
ACOLI*	5	10	15	20	25	30	40	50	60
0%	$1,000	$1,000	$1,000	$1,000	$1,000	$1,000	$1,000	$1,000	$1,000
1	$1,041	$1,094	$1,149	$1,208	$1,270	$1,334	$1,474	$1,628	$1,799
2	$1,082	$1,195	$1,319	$1,457	$1,608	$1,776	$2,165	$2,639	$3,217
3	$1,125	$1,305	$1,513	$1,753	$2,033	$2,357	$3,167	$4,256	$5,720
4	$1,170	$1,423	$1,732	$2,107	$2,563	$3,119	$4,616	$6,833	$10,115
5	$1,215	$1,551	$1,980	$2,527	$3,225	$4,116	$6,705	$10,921	$17,790
6	$1,267	$1,689	$2,261	$3,026	$4,049	$5,418	$9,704	$17,378	$31,120
7	$1,311	$1,838	$2,578	$3,617	$5,072	$7,114	$13,995	$27,530	$54,156
8	$1,360	$1,999	$2,937	$4,316	$6,341	$9,317	$20,115	$43,427	$93,757

*ACOLI = Annual Cost of Living Increase

Appendix B:

"PRESENT (CURRENT) VALUE" OF FUTURE AMOUNT

PVS-1: Calculates the amount of investment needed at the beginning of the year to be worth the future value for the year indicated.

PVS-1: Assumes the investment needed to be worth $1,000 in the future.

TABLE PVS-1									
	YEARS INTO THE FUTURE UNTIL THE AMOUNT IS RECEIVED								
ROR*	5	10	15	20	25	30	40	50	60
0%	$1,000	$1,000	$1,000	$1,000	$1,000	$1,000	$1,000	$1,000	$1,000
1	$951	$905	$861	$820	$780	$742	$672	$608	$550
2	$906	$820	$743	$673	$609	$552	$453	$372	$305
3	$863	$744	$642	$554	$478	$412	$307	$228	$170
4	$822	$676	$555	$456	$375	$308	$208	$141	$95
5	$784	$614	$481	$377	$295	$231	$142	$87	$54
6	$747	$558	$417	$312	$233	$174	$97	$54	$30
7	$713	$508	$362	$258	$184	$131	$67	$34	$17
8	$681	$463	$315	$215	$146	$99	$46	$21	$10

*ROR = Rate of Return

WHEN TO USE PVS-1: When you expect to receive monies (or assets) in the future and want to know what they would be "worth" in current dollars (i.e.: the amount to invest now at a specified rate of return to be worth that amount at a specified number of years in the future). For example, you expect to receive $50,000 in 10 years and want to know what it would be worth today if the money were invested earning 4% per year between now and then.

HOW TO USE PVS-1: Once you choose the number of years (column) until the funds would be received, and the average rate of return (row) money invested now would earn during those years, find the value where the column/row intersect. This value is your "present value multiplier." Since the values in the table are based on an initial amount of $1,000, divide the expected future amount by $1,000 to calculate the "investment multiplier." Multiply the "present value multiplier" by the "investment multiplier" to calculate the current investment needed.

TEST YOURSELF USING PVS-1: Assume you will receive an inheritance of $250,000 in 30 years. How much would you need to invest today to be worth $250,000 in 30 years if your investments earn 8% / year? (Answer: $24,750).

PVS-2 calculates the income needed at the beginning of the current year to be worth the specified future income for the year indicated.

PVS-2 assumes the future income needed is $1,000 a year.

TABLE PVS-2									
YEARS INTO THE FUTURE UNTIL THE AMOUNT IS RECEIVED									
ACOLI*	5	10	15	20	25	30	40	50	60
0%	$1,000	$1,000	$1,000	$1,000	$1,000	$1,000	$1,000	$1,000	$1,000
1	$961	$914	$870	$828	$788	$749	$678	$614	$556
2	$924	$837	$758	$686	$622	$563	$462	$379	$311
3	$888	$766	$661	$570	$492	$424	$316	$235	$175
4	$855	$703	$577	$475	$390	$321	$217	$146	$99
5	$823	$645	$505	$396	$310	$243	$149	$92	$56
6	$792	$592	$442	$331	$247	$185	$103	$58	$32
7	$763	$544	$388	$277	$197	$141	$71	$36	$18
8	$735	$500	$340	$232	$158	$107	$50	$23	$11

*ACOLI = Annual Cost of Living Increase

WHEN TO USE PVS-2: When you know an amount of income to be received a specific number of years in the future, and want to know, adjusted for inflation, its worth in current dollars. For example, your social security benefits will be $1,000 per month starting in 50 years and you want to know what those benefits would be worth in current purchasing power adjusted for inflation of 5% per year.

HOW TO USE PVS-2: Once you choose the number of years (Column) until benefits will be received, and the average inflation rate (row) assumed, find the value where column / row intersect. This value is your "present cost multiplier." Since values in the table are based on an initial amount of $1,000, divide the projected future benefit by $1,000 to calculate the "income multiplier." Multiply the "present cost multiplier" by the "income multiplier" to calculate the current income equivalent.

TEST YOURSELF USING PVS-2: Assume you will be receiving a pension of $2,000 a month starting 25 years from now. If the cost of living increases 4% / year, how much would that future $2,000 be worth in current dollars? (Answer: $780 a month)

Appendix C:

FUTURE VALUE OF ANNUAL INVESTMENTS

- Values provided are based on an initial amount of $1,000.
- AIIPY = Annual Investment Increase Per Year

All tables in Appendix C assume the annual investment is made at the end of each year, and the value in the table represents the accumulated value at the end of the indicated year.

WHEN TO USE TABLES FVA-0, FVA-1, FVA-3, and FVA-5: When you plan to make annual investments and want to know what those investments would be worth if made for a specified number of years earning a specified assumed rate of return per year on the invested funds.

The difference between the 4 tables provided are as follows:

- The values in table FVA-0 are based on a fixed annual investment of $1,000 a year for the period specified.
- The values in table FVA-1 assume an initial annual investment of $1,000, increasing 1% a year through the period specified.
- The values in table FVA-3 assume an initial annual investment of $1,000, increasing 3% a year through the period specified.
- The values in table FVA-5 assume an initial annual investment of $1,000, increasing 5% a year through the period specified.

HOW TO USE TABLES FVA-0, FVA-1, FVA-3, and FVA-5: The correct table to use is based on the percent you plan to increase your investments each year during the specified investment period. Tables are provided for annual increases of 1% (FVA-1), 3% (FVA-3), and 5% (FVA-5), as well as if a fixed annual investment is planned (FVA-0). If you will be increasing your annual investment amount by different percentages during the investment period (for example increase 3% for 10 years, then by 1% for another 5 years), you will need to process the calculation in segments.

Once you have decided on the number of years you plan to be investing, and the rate of return those funds are assumed to earn, you would use the applicable "increase per year" table to select the value where the years and assumed investment rate of return (ROR) intersect. This value is your "accumulated value multiplier." Because the values in the table are based on an initial annual investment of $1,000, to calculate the "investment multiplier" you would divide the actual initial investment amount by $1,000. Then multiply the "accumulated value multiplier" by the "investment multiplier" to calculate the future value of your actual investment.

For example, assume you plan to increase your investment amount 1% a year. You would use Table FVA-1. If the initial investment planned is $5,000, you plan to make an annual investment for a total of 20 years, and assume the investments will earn 6% a year, the value from Table FVA-1 that you would use as the "accumulated value multiplier" is $39,739. Since the planned initial investment is $5,000, divided by $1,000 results in an "investment multiplier" of 5. That means in 20 years, the value of this referenced investment would be 5 × $39,739 = $198,695.

Using the same initial $5,000 a year, 20 year investment time frame, and an investment return of 6% a year, the values based on

- No increase a year = 5 x $36,786 = $183,930

- 3% increase a year = 5 x $46,701 = $233,505

- 5% increase a year = 5 x $55,384 = $276,920

FVA–0: To calculate the future value of a series of annual FIXED investments. This assumes $1,000 per year as the initial annual amount.

TABLE FVA-0									
AIIPY 0%	YEARS ANNUAL INVESTMENT WILL BE MADE								
ROR*	5	10	15	20	25	30	40	50	60
0%	$5,000	$10,000	$15,000	$20,000	$25,000	$30,000	$40,000	$50,000	$60,000
1	$5,101	$10,462	$16,097	$22,019	$28,243	$34,785	$48,886	$64,463	$81,670
2	$5,204	$10,950	$17,293	$24,297	$32,030	$40,568	$60,402	$84,579	$114,052
3	$5,309	$11,464	$18,599	$26,870	$36,459	$47,575	$75,401	$112,797	$163,053
4	$5,416	$12,006	$20,024	$29,778	$41,646	$56,085	$95,026	$152,667	$237,991
5	$5,526	$12,578	$21,579	$33,066	$47,727	$66,439	$120,800	$209,348	$353,584
6	$5,637	$13,181	$23,276	$36,786	$54,865	$79,058	$154,762	$290,335	$533,128
7	$5,751	$13,816	$25,129	$40,995	$63,249	$94,461	$199,635	$406,529	$813,520
8	$5,867	$14,487	$27,152	$45,762	$73,106	$113,283	$259,057	$573,770	$1,253,213

*ROR = Rate of Return

AN EXAMPLE TO TEST YOURSELF USING FVA-0: Assume the annual investment amount is $15,000, the assumed investment rate of return is 6%, and you want to know what that investment would be worth in 20 years. (Answer: $36,786 x 15 = $551,790)

FVA–1: To calculate the future value of a series of annual investments in which the amount invested is increased 1% a year. This assumes $1,000 per year as the initial annual amount

TABLE FVA-1

AIIPY 1%	YEARS ANNUAL INVESTMENT WILL BE MADE								
ROR*	5	10	15	20	25	30	40	50	60
0%	$5,101	$10,462	$16,097	$22,019	$28,243	$34,789	$48,886	$64,463	$81,670
1	$5,203	$10,937	$17,242	$24,163	$31,743	$40,035	$58,965	$81,417	$107,923
2	$5,307	$11,437	$18,490	$26,576	$35,817	$46,351	$71,918	$104,696	$146,433
3	$5,413	$11,965	$19,850	$29,296	$40,567	$53,971	$88,659	$136,964	$203,745
4	$5,521	$12,521	$21,332	$32,364	$46,113	$63,185	$110,405	$182,068	$290,098
5	$5,632	$13,107	$22,949	$35,828	$52,598	$74,352	$138,778	$245,569	$421,562
6	$5,744	$13,725	$24,712	$39,739	$60,189	$87,913	$175,937	$335,510	$623,420
7	$5,859	$14,375	$26,634	$44,158	$69,083	$104,407	$224,760	$463,540	$935,496
8	$5,976	$15,061	$28,731	$49,154	$79,515	$124,497	$289,081	$646,528	$1,420,577

*ROR = Rate of Return

AN EXAMPLE TO TEST YOURSELF USING FVA-1: Assume the initial investment amount is $12,000, it increases 1% a year, the assumed investment rate of return is 4%, and you want to know what that investment would be worth in 25 years. (Answer: $46,113 x 12 = $553,356)

FVA–3: To calculate the future value of a series of annual investments in which the amount invested is increased 3% a year. This assumes $1,000 per year as the initial annual amount.

TABLE FVA-3

AIIPY 3%	YEARS ANNUAL INVESTMENT WILL BE MADE								
ROR*	5	10	15	20	25	30	40	50	60
0%	$5,309	$11,464	$18,599	$26,870	$36,459	$47,575	$75,401	$112,797	$163,053
1	$5,413	$11,965	$19,850	$29,296	$40,567	$53,971	$88,659	$136,964	$203,745
2	$5,519	$12,492	$21,210	$32,016	$45,317	$61,590	$105,400	$169,232	$261,057
3	$5,628	$13,048	$22,689	$35,070	$50,820	$70,697	$126,681	$212,811	$343,200
4	$5,738	$13,633	$24,298	$38,501	$57,206	$81,614	$153,898	$272,278	$462,802
5	$5,850	$14,249	$26,048	$42,359	$64,629	$94,734	$188,898	$354,175	$639,379
6	$5,965	$14,898	$27,953	$46,701	$73,270	$110,541	$234,123	$467,875	$903,203
7	$6,082	$15,581	$30,027	$51,589	$83,341	$129,625	$292,811	$626,828	$1,301,370
8	$6,201	$16,300	$32,284	$57,097	$95,094	$152,708	$369,250	$850,354	$1,907,309

*ROR = Rate of Return

AN EXAMPLE TO TEST YOURSELF USING FVA-3: Assume the initial investment amount is $20,000, it will be increased 3% a year, the assumed investment rate of return is 6%, and you want to know what that investment would be worth in 15 years. (Answer: $27,953 x 20 = $559,060)

FVA–5: To calculate the future value of a series of annual investments in which the amount invested is increased 5% a year. This assumes $1,000 per year as the initial annual amount.

TABLE FVA-5

AIIPY 5%	YEARS ANNUAL INVESTMENT WILL BE MADE								
ROR*	5	10	15	20	25	30	40	50	60
0%	$5,526	$12,578	$21,579	$33,066	$47,727	$66,439	$120,800	$209,348	$353,584
1	$5,632	$13,107	$22,949	$35,828	$52,598	$74,352	$138,778	$245,569	$421,562
2	$5,740	$13,663	$24,435	$38,912	$58,192	$83,686	$161,065	$292,527	$513,272
3	$5,850	$14,249	$26,048	$42,359	$64,629	$94,734	$188,898	$354,175	$639,379
4	$5,963	$14,865	$27,798	$46,217	$72,052	$107,854	$223,897	$436,071	$815,956
5	$6,078	$15,513	$29,699	$50,539	$80,627	$123,484	$268,190	$546,067	$1,067,382
6	$6,194	$16,195	$31,763	$55,384	$90,552	$142,155	$324,573	$695,275	$1,430,850
7	$6,314	$16,913	$34,005	$60,819	$102,054	$164,516	$396,723	$899,481	$1,963,362
8	$6,435	$17,668	$36,441	$66,922	$115,404	$191,357	$489,484	$1,181,140	$2,752,596

*ROR = Rate of Return

AN EXAMPLE TO TEST YOURSELF USING FVA-5: Assume the investment amount is $5,000, it will be increased 5% a year, the assumed investment rate of return is 7%, and you want to know what that investment would be worth in 40 years. (Answer: $396,723 x 5 = $1,983,615)

Appendix D:

INVESTMENT NEEDED TO GENERATE / WITHDRAW FUTURE ANNUAL INCOME / BENEFIT (What is technically known as the present value of an annuity.)

- Values provided are based on an initial amount of $1,000 a year.
- AWIPY = Annual Withdrawal Increase Per Year
- ROR = Rate of Return

All tables in Appendix D assume the annual withdrawal to be made or the benefit to be received occurs at the start of each year and the last annual withdrawal / benefit lasts for the years being specified.

WHEN TO USE TABLES PVA-0, PVA-1, PVA-3, and PVA-5:

When you want to calculate the amount to be invested at a specified rate of return to be able to withdraw a specified annual amount each year for the years indicated (must be at least 2 years), or that would need to be invested to replace a specified annual amount of benefits (*such as social security, pension, mortgage income*) expected to be received over multiple years.

HOW TO USE TABLES PVA-0, PVA-1, PVA-3, and PVA-5:

The correct table to use is based on the percent you plan to increase your withdrawals each year during the specified withdrawal period, or the expected annual increase in benefits to be received during the specified payment period.

Tables are provided to calculate a fixed annual withdrawal/benefit (PVA-0), as well as withdrawals / benefits assuming annual increases of 1% (PVA-1), 3% (PVA-3) and 5% (PVA-5). If your annual withdrawal or benefit amount will increase by different percentages during the withdrawal period (for example increase 3% for 10 years, followed by 1% for another 5 years), you will need to process the calculation in segments.

Once you choose the number of years the withdrawal will be made / benefits will be received (column) and the rate of return (row) the calculated investment is assumed to earn, you would use the applicable "increase per year" table to select the value where the years for withdrawal (column) and assumed rate of return on the invested amount (row) intersect. This is your "investment needed multiplier."

Since the values in the table are based on an initial annual withdrawal / benefit of $1,000, to calculate the "withdrawal multiplier" you would divide the actual withdrawal amount by $1,000. Then multiply the "investment needed multiplier" by the "withdrawal multiplier" to calculate the investment amount needed to fund the specified withdrawal / benefit for the period indicated.

For example, assume you plan to increase your withdrawal amount 1% a year. You would use Table PVA-1. If the initial withdrawal planned is $5,000, and you want to make withdrawals for 20 years, assuming the investment return (*technically known as the "discount rate"*) will be 6% a year, the value from Table PVA-1 you would use as the "investment value multiplier" is $13,134. Since the planned initial investment is $5,000, divided by $1,000 results in a "withdrawal multiplier" of 5. That means to make the specified annual withdrawals for 20 years, the investment amount needed would be 5 x $13,134 = $65,671.

Using the same initial $5,000 a year, 20-year investment time frame and an investment return of 6% a year, the values based on

- No increase a year = 5 x $12,158 = $60,790

- 3% increase a year = 5 x $15,435 = $77,175

- 5% increase a year = 5 x $18,305 = $91,525

An important use of this Appendix is evaluating the choice between taking a pension as a lump sum or lifetime income.

Suppose you are required to choose between receiving a lump sum of $150,000 or a lifetime pension of $12,000 a year. You assume a conservative investment portfolio will earn 3% a year. If the $150,000 invested at 3% can realistically generate more than $12,000 a year for your projected life expectancy, the lump sum is a better choice; if not, the pension would be a "wealthier" choice.

A key determining factor in this calculation is the number of years you expect to be alive to collect the pension.

Since the pension is assumed to be fixed (*the same amount each year*), Table PVA-0 would be used.

For a life expectancy of 10 years (column) and a 3% discount rate (row), the "investment value multiplier" would be $8,786. Since the table assumes an annual amount of $1,000, and your proposed pension is $12,000, to get the "withdrawal multiplier," you would divide $12,000 by $1,000 = 12. $8,786 x 12 = $105,432. Which means you would need $105,432 invested at 3% to withdraw $12,000 a year for 10 years.

For 20 years, the "investment value multiplier" is $15,324, the "withdrawal multiplier" is 12. $15,324 x 12 = $183,888. Which means if your investments earn 3% a year, and you want to be able to withdraw $12,000 a year for 20 years, the lump sum equivalent would be $183,888.

Since you were offered a lump sum of $150,000, if you expected to live for 10 years, you would do better taking the lump sum, however if you expected to live for 20 years, the pension would be the "wealthier" choice.

To help you better "see" this, the table titled "Pension Vs. Lump Sum Analysis" shows the annual withdrawal and the remaining balance for investments of $150,000 (the offered lump sum) as well as the amount equivalent to 10 years of the offered pension ($105,432) and 20 years of the offered pension ($183,888).

PENSION VS. LUMP SUM ANALYSIS

Starting balance		$150,000	$105,432	$183,888
Year	Annual withdrawal	Remaining balance	Remaining balance	Remaining balance
1	$12,000	$142,140	$96,235	$177,045
2	$12,000	$134,044	$86,762	$169,996
3	$12,000	$125,706	$77,005	$162,736
4	$12,000	$117,117	$66,955	$155,258
5	$12,000	$108,270	$56,604	$147,556
6	$12,000	$99,158	$45,942	$139,622
7	$12,000	$89,773	$34,960	$131,451
8	$12,000	$80,106	$23,649	$123,035
9	$12,000	$70,149	$11,998	$114,366
10	$12,000	$59,894	-$2	$105,437
11	$12,000	$49,331		$96,240
12	$12,000	$38,451		$86,767
13	$12,000	$27,244		$77,010
14	$12,000	$15,701		$66,960
15	$12,000	$3,813		$56,609
16	$12,000			$45,947
17	$12,000			$34,966
18	$12,000			$23,655
19	$12,000			$12,004
20	$12,000			$4

PVA–0: The investment amount needed to withdraw a FIXED amount. This assumes $1,000 / year as base amount.

TABLE PVA-0									
AWIPY 0%	YEARS ANNUAL WITHDRAWAL WILL BE MADE								
ROR*	5	10	15	20	25	30	40	50	60
0%	$5,000	$10,000	$15,000	$20,000	$25,000	$30,000	$40,000	$50,000	$60,000
1	$4,902	$9,566	$14,004	$18,226	$22,243	$26,066	$33,163	$39,588	$45,405
2	$4,808	$9,162	$13,106	$16,678	$19,914	$22,844	$27,903	$32,052	$35,456
3	$4,717	$8,786	$12,296	$15,324	$17,936	$20,188	$23,808	$26,502	$28,505
4	$4,630	$8,435	$11,563	$14,134	$16,247	$17,984	$20,584	$22,341	$23,528
5	$4,546	$8,108	$10,899	$13,085	$14,799	$16,141	$18,017	$19,169	$19,876
6	$4,465	$7,802	$10,295	$12,158	$13,550	$14,591	$15,949	$16,708	$17,131
7	$4,387	$7,515	$9,745	$11,336	$12,469	$13,278	$14,265	$14,767	$15,022
8	$4,312	$7,247	$9,244	$10,604	$11,529	$12,158	$12,879	$13,212	$13,367

ROR = Rate of Return

EXAMPLES TO TEST YOURSELF USING PVA-0:

- You are expecting a fixed pension of $10,000 a year and want to know what that future income is worth in "retirement dollars" if you expect to live for 20 years and assumed the discount rate is 4% a year. (Answer: $14,134 x 10 = $141,340)

- You are holding a mortgage for which you will receive $5,000 a year for another 10 years, assume a discount rate of 5% a year and want to know what that future income is worth in "investment dollars." (Answer: $8,108 x 5 = $40,540)

PVA–1: The investment amount needed to withdraw a 1% annually increasing amount. This assumes $1,000 / year as base amount.

TABLE PVA-1									
AWIPY 1%	YEARS ANNUAL WITHDRAWAL WILL BE MADE								
ROR*	5	10	15	20	25	30	40	50	60
0%	$5,101	$10,462	$16,097	$22,019	$28,243	$34,789	$48,886	$64,463	$81,670
1	$5,000	$10,000	$15,000	$20,000	$25,000	$30,000	$40,000	$50,000	$60,000
2	$4,903	$9,570	$14,013	$18,242	$22,268	$26,101	$33,222	$39,675	$45,523
3	$4,810	$9,170	$13,123	$16,707	$19,956	$22,902	$27,994	$32,180	$35,620
4	$4,720	$8,797	$12,319	$15,362	$17,990	$20,260	$23,916	$26,644	$28,680
5	$4,633	$8,449	$11,591	$14,178	$16,309	$18,063	$20,698	$22,485	$23,697
6	$4,550	$8,124	$10,930	$13,134	$14,865	$16,224	$18,131	$19,307	$20,032
7	$4,470	$7,819	$10,329	$12,210	$13,620	$14,676	$16,060	$16,838	$17,274
8	$4,393	$7,534	$9,782	$11,390	$12,539	$13,362	$14,371	$14,888	$15,152

*ROR = Rate of Return

AN EXAMPLE TO TEST YOURSELF USING PVA-1:

- You are expecting an initial social security benefit of $10,000 a year and benefits increasing 1% a year and want to know how much that future income is worth in "retirement dollars" if you expect to live for 20 years and assumed the discount rate is 4% a year. (Answer: $15,362 x 10 = $153,620)

PVA–3: The investment amount needed to withdraw a 3% annually increasing amount. This assumes $1,000 / year as base amount.

TABLE PVA-3

AWIPY 3%	YEARS ANNUAL WITHDRAWAL WILL BE MADE								
ROR*	5	10	15	20	25	30	40	50	60
0%	$5,309	$11,464	$18,599	$26,870	$36,459	$47,575	$75,401	$112,797	$163,053
1	$5,202	$10,940	$17,269	$24,250	$31,949	$40,443	$60,143	$84,112	$113,273
2	$5,099	$10,453	$16,074	$21,977	$28,175	$34,682	$48,689	$64,132	$81,157
3	$5,000	$10,000	$15,000	$20,000	$25,000	$30,000	$40,000	$50,000	$60,000
4	$4,905	$9,578	$14,031	$18,274	$22,317	$26,169	$33,338	$39,845	$45,754
5	$4,813	$9,185	$13,156	$16,763	$20,039	$23,015	$28,174	$32,430	$35,941
6	$4,725	$8,818	$12,364	$15,435	$18,096	$20,401	$24,128	$26,924	$29,023
7	$4,640	$8,475	$11,645	$14,265	$16,430	$18,220	$20,923	$22,769	$24,030
8	$4,558	$8,154	$10,991	$13,230	$14,996	$16,390	$18,357	$19,581	$20,343

*ROR = Rate of Return

AN EXAMPLE TO TEST YOURSELF USING PVA-3:

- You are expecting an initial social security benefit of $10,000 a year increasing 3% a year and want to know how much that future income is worth in "retirement dollars" if you expect to live for 20 years and assumed the discount rate is 4% a year. (Answer: $18,274 x 10 = $182,740)

PVA–5: The investment amount needed to withdraw a 5% annually increasing amount. This assumes $1,000 / year as base amount.

TABLE PVA-5

AWIPY 5%	YEARS ANNUAL WITHDRAWAL WILL BE MADE								
ROR*	5	10	15	20	25	30	40	50	60
0%	$5,526	$12,578	$21,579	$33,066	$47,727	$66,439	$120,800	$209,348	$353,584
1	$5,412	$11,984	$19,965	$29,656	$41,424	$55,715	$94,143	$150,809	$234,369
2	$5,303	$11,433	$18,519	$26,710	$36,179	$47,125	$74,404	$110,856	$159,565
3	$5,198	$10,921	$17,221	$24,157	$31,793	$40,200	$59,645	$83,213	$110,780
4	$5,097	$10,444	$16,053	$21,937	$28,109	$34,584	$48,501	$63,815	$80,668
5	$5,000	$10,000	$15,000	$20,000	$25,000	$30,000	$40,000	$50,000	$60,000
6	$4,907	$9,586	$14,049	$18,305	$22,364	$26,236	$33,449	$40,010	$45,978
7	$4,816	$9,199	$13,188	$16,817	$20,120	$23,125	$28,348	$32,673	$36,254
8	$4,730	$8,838	$12,407	$15,507	$18,199	$20,538	$24,334	$27,198	$29,359

*ROR = Rate of Return

AN EXAMPLE TO TEST YOURSELF USING PVA-5:

- You are expecting an initial social security benefit of $10,000 a year increasing 5% a year and want to know how much that future income is worth in "retirement dollars" if you expect to live for 20 years and assumed the discount rate is 4% a year. (Answer: $21,937 x 10 = $219,370)

Appendix E:

CALCULATING THE INITIAL ANNUAL WITHDRAWAL
Based on a specified amount of investment.

- Calculations are based on an available investment amount of $10,000.
- AWIPY = annual withdrawal increase per year.

All tables in Appendix E assume the annual withdrawal to be made occurs at the start of each year and the annual withdrawal / benefit lasts for the totals years being specified.

These tables assume funds are depleted at the end of the years for withdrawal that are used.

WHEN TO USE TABLES IWA-0, IWA-1, IWA-3, and IWA-5:

When you have a specified amount of money available to be invested from which you will make annual withdrawals based on a specified number of years for the withdrawals to last, and a specified rate of return on the funds invested, and you want to calculate the amount you could withdraw in year 1 that would allow your funds to last the years indicated.

NOTE: Tables in Appendix D, and Appendix E may look similar, however in Appendix D, you know the initial withdrawal wanted, and want to calculate the investment needed (PVA = present value annuity) to support those withdrawals, and in Appendix E the available investment amount is known and you want to calculate the allowed Year 1 withdrawal (IWA = initial withdrawal amount).

HOW TO USE TABLES IWA-0, IWA-1, IWA-3, and IWA-5:

(IMPORTANT REMINDER: INVESTMENT AVAILABLE WILL BE **DIVIDED** *by $10,000 TO CALCULATE "annual withdrawal multiplier")*

The correct table to use is based on the percent you plan to increase your withdrawals each year during the specified withdrawal period.

Tables are provided to calculate a fixed annual withdrawal (IWA-0), as well as withdrawals assuming annual increases of 1% (IWA-1), 3% (IWA-3) and 5% (IWA-5). If your annual withdrawal amount will increase by different percentages during the withdrawal period (for example increase 3% for 10 years, followed by 1% for another 5 years), you will need to process the calculation in segments.

Once you choose the number of years the withdrawal will be made (column) and the rate of return (row) the available investment is assumed to earn, you would use the applicable "increase per year" table to select the value where the years for withdrawal (column) and assumed rate of return on the invested amount (row) intersect. This is your "withdrawal multiplier."

Since the values in the table are based on an Investment of $10,000, to calculate the "investment amount multiplier" you would divide the investment amount by $10,000. Then multiply the "investment amount multiplier" by the "withdrawal multiplier" to calculate the investment amount needed to fund the specified withdrawal for the period indicated.

For example, assume you plan to increase your withdrawal amount 3% a year. You would use Table IWA-3. If the investment amount available to withdraw from is $250,000 and you want to make withdrawals for 20 years, assuming the investment return (*technically known as the "discount rate"*) will be 5% a year, the value from Table IWA-3 you would use as the "withdrawal multiplier" is $597. Since the investment amount is $250,000, divided by $10,000 results in a "withdrawal multiplier" of 25. That means the initial withdrawal for year 1 would be $597 x 25 = $14,925, with the withdrawal amount increasing 3% each year.

Using the same initial $250,000 investment, a 20-year investment time frame and an investment return of 5% a year, the initial withdrawal would be

- 25 x $764 = $19,100 with no annual increase in withdrawals
- 25 x $705 = $17,625 with a 3% annual increase in withdrawals
- 25 x $500 = $12,500 with a 5% annual increase in withdrawals

A NOTE: I encourage you to review the example provided using IWA-0 and IWA-5. The only difference in the assumptions made is that in IWA-0, the withdrawal is the same each year, and in IWA-5 the withdrawal is assumed to increase 5% a year, but the initial withdrawal amount is much different.

IWA–0: Calculate the first in a series of fixed annual withdrawals from a specified invested amount. This assumes an initial $10,000 investment.

TABLE IWA-0									
AWIPY 0%	NUMBER OF YEARS FUNDS NEED TO LAST								
ROR*	5	10	15	20	25	30	40	50	60
0%	$2,000	$1,000	$667	$500	$400	$333	$250	$200	$167
1	$2,040	$1,045	$714	$549	$450	$384	$302	$253	$220
2	$2,080	$1,091	$763	$600	$502	$438	$358	$312	$282
3	$2,120	$1,138	$813	$653	$558	$495	$420	$377	$351
4	$2,160	$1,185	$865	$708	$615	$556	$486	$448	$425
5	$2,200	$1,233	$918	$764	$676	$620	$555	$522	$503
6	$2,240	$1,282	$971	$822	$738	$685	$627	$599	$584
7	$2,279	$1,331	$1,026	$882	$802	$753	$701	$677	$666
8	$2,319	$1,380	$1,082	$943	$867	$822	$776	$757	$748

*ROR = Rate of Return

AN EXAMPLE TO TEST YOURSELF USING IWA-0 Your retirement account is worth $300,000. You expect to live 30 years and want to know how much you could withdraw each year for the rest of your life if the money earned 4% a year and you withdrew the same amount each year. (ANSWER: $556 x 30 = $16,680)

IWA–1: Calculate the first in a series of annual withdrawals increasing 1% a year from a specified invested amount. Assumes an initial $10,000 invested.

TABLE IWA-1

AWIPY 1%	NUMBER OF YEARS FUNDS NEED TO LAST								
ROR*	5	10	15	20	25	30	40	50	60
0%	$1,960	$956	$621	$454	$354	$287	$205	$155	$122
1	$2,000	$1,000	$667	$500	$400	$333	$250	$200	$167
2	$2,040	$1,045	$714	$548	$449	$383	$301	$252	$220
3	$2,079	$1,091	$762	$599	$501	$437	$357	$311	$281
4	$2,119	$1,137	$812	$651	$556	$494	$418	$375	$349
5	$2,158	$1,184	$863	$705	$613	$554	$483	$445	$422
6	$2,198	$1,231	$915	$761	$673	$616	$552	$518	$499
7	$2,237	$1,279	$968	$819	$734	$681	$623	$594	$579
8	$2,277	$1,327	$1,022	$878	$797	$758	$696	$672	$660

*ROR = Rate of Return

AN EXAMPLE TO TEST YOURSELF USING IWA-1 You receive an accident settlement worth $200,000. You expect to live 20 years and want to know how much you could withdraw each year for the rest of your life if the money earned 3% a year and you increased your withdrawal 1% each year. (ANSWER: $599 x 20 = $11,980)

IWA–3: Calculate the first in a series of annual withdrawals increasing 3% a year from a specified invested amount. Assumes an initial $10,000 invested.

TABLE IWA-3

AWIPY 3%	NUMBER OF YEARS FUNDS NEED TO LAST								
ROR*	5	10	15	20	25	30	40	50	60
0%	$1,884	$872	$538	$372	$274	$210	$133	$89	$61
1	$1,922	$914	$579	$412	$313	$247	$166	$119	$88
2	$1,961	$957	$622	$455	$355	$288	$205	$156	$123
3	$2,000	$1,000	$667	$500	$400	$333	$250	$200	$167
4	$2,039	$1,044	$713	$547	$448	$382	$300	$251	$219
5	$2,077	$1,089	$760	$597	$499	$434	$355	$308	$278
6	$2,116	$1,134	$809	$648	$553	$490	$414	$371	$345
7	$2,155	$1,108	$859	$701	$609	$549	$478	$439	$416
8	$2,194	$1,226	$910	$756	$667	$610	$545	$511	$492

*ROR = Rate of Return

AN EXAMPLE TO TEST YOURSELF USING IWA-3 Your retirement account is worth $500,000. You expect to live 40 years and want to know how much you could withdraw each year for the rest of your life if the money earned 5% a year and your withdrawals are increased by 3% a year. (ANSWER: $355 x 50 = $17,750)

IWA–5: Calculate the first in a series of annual withdrawals increasing 5% a year from a specified invested amount. Assumes an initial $10,000 invested.

TABLE IWA-5									
AWIPY 5%	NUMBER OF YEARS FUNDS NEED TO LAST								
ROR*	5	10	15	20	25	30	40	50	60
0%	$1,810	$795	$463	$302	$210	$151	$83	$48	$28
1	$1,848	$834	$501	$337	$241	$179	$106	$66	$43
2	$1,886	$875	$540	$374	$276	$212	$134	$90	$63
3	$1,924	$916	$581	$414	$315	$249	$168	$120	$89
4	$1,962	$957	$623	$456	$356	$289	$206	$157	$124
5	$2,000	$1,000	$667	$500	$400	$333	$250	$200	$167
6	$2,038	$1,043	$712	$546	$447	$381	$299	$250	$217
7	$2,076	$1,087	$758	$595	$497	$432	$353	$306	$276
8	$2,114	$1,131	$806	$645	$549	$487	$411	$368	$341

*ROR = Rate of Return

AN EXAMPLE TO TEST YOURSELF USING IWA-5 Your retirement account is worth $300,000. You expect to live 30 years and want to know how much you could withdraw each year for the rest of your life if the money earned 4% a year and you increased your withdrawals by 5% a year. (ANSWER: $289 x 30 = $8,670)

Appendix F:

INITIAL INVESTMENT AMOUNT NEEDED

- Values provided are based on an initial investment amount of $1.00 per year.
- AIIPY = Annual Investment Increase per Year
- ROR = Rate Of Return

The tables in Appendix F assume an initial annual investment of $1.00 made at the beginning of the year.

WHEN TO USE TABLES IIA-0, IIA-1, IIA-3, and IIA-5: When you have a desired amount to accumulate in a specified number of years in the future, and want to calculate the initial annual investment needed at a specified rate of return to accumulate that amount.

HOW TO USE TABLES IIA-0, IIA-1, IIA-3, and IIA-5: The correct table to use is based on the percent you plan to increase your investment each year during the specified investment period.

Tables are provided to calculate a fixed annual investment (IIA-0), as well as the initial annual investment assuming annual increases of 1% (IIA-1), 3% (IIA-3) and 5% (IIA-5). If your annual investment will increase by different percentages during the investment period (for example increase 3% for 10 years, followed by 1% for another 5 years), you will need to process the calculation in segments.

Once you choose the years the investments will be made (column) and the rate of return (row) the investments are assumed to earn, you would use the applicable "increase per year" table to select the value where the years annual investments will be made (column) and assumed rate of return on the invested amount (row)intersect. This is your "investment needed multiplier."

Since the values in the table are based on an initial annual investment of $1.00, all you would need to do is divide the desired future amount by the "investment needed multiplier" to calculate the annual investment amount needed to accumulate the specified future amount in the period specified.

For example: Suppose you wanted to accumulate $100,000 in 10 years, planned to invest the same amount each year and each year's investment would earn 4% per year. You would use Table IIA-0 (no increase in investment amount). The divisor from the table would be where 10 years and 4% ROR intersect. That value is $12.00. $100,000 divided by $12.00 = $8,333.33 (rounded to $8,333). Which means if you invested $8,333 a year earning 4% a year for 10 years, you would accumulate $100,000. The table below shows this on a year by year basis.

$100,000 IN 10 YEARS AT 4%

Year	Amount invested	Cumulative value at 4%
1	$8,333	8,333
2	$8,333	16,999
3	$8,333	26,012
4	$8,333	35,386
5	$8,333	45,134
6	$8,333	55,273
7	$8,333	65,816
8	$8,333	76,782
9	$8,333	88,186
10	$8,333	100,047

Using the same initial $100,000 future value, 10-year investment period and rate of return of 4% a year, the initial investment needed based on:

- 1% increase a year = $100,000 / 12.52 = $7,987
- 3% increase a year = $100,000 / 13.63 = $7,337
- 5% increase a year = $100,000 / 14.87 = $6,725

IIA–0: This table assumes no annual increase in the investment amount (AIIPY = 0).

TABLE IIA-0

0% AIIPY	YEARS ANNUAL INVESTMENT WILL BE MADE								
ROR*	5	10	15	20	25	30	40	50	60
0%	5.00	10.00	15.00	20.00	25.00	30.00	40.00	50.00	60.00
1	5.10	10.46	16.10	22.02	28.24	34.78	48.89	64.46	81.67
2	5.20	10.95	17.29	24.30	32.03	40.57	60.40	84.58	114.05
3	5.31	11.46	18.60	26.87	36.46	47.58	75.40	112.80	163.05
4	5.42	12.00	20.02	29.78	41.65	56.08	95.02	152.67	237.99
5	5.53	12.58	21.58	33.07	47.73	66.44	120.80	209.35	353.58
6	5.64	13.18	23.28	36.79	54.86	79.06	154.76	290.34	533.13
7	5.75	13.82	25.13	41.00	63.25	94.46	199.64	406.53	813.52
8	5.87	14.49	27.15	45.76	73.11	113.28	259.06	573.77	1253.21

*ROR = Rate of Return

AN EXAMPLE TO TEST YOURSELF USING IIA-0: You want to accumulate $50,000 in 20 years and want to know how much you would need to invest each year if you invested the same amount each year and your investments earned 5% a year. (ANSWER: $50,000 / 33.07 = $1,512)

IIA–1: This table assumes the annual investment amount will increase 1% per year (AIIPY = 1).

TABLE IIA-1									
1% AIIPY	YEARS ANNUAL INVESTMENT WILL BE MADE								
ROR*	5	10	15	20	25	30	40	50	60
0%	5.10	10.46	16.10	22.02	28.24	34.79	48.89	64.46	81.67
1	5.20	10.94	17.24	24.16	31.74	40.03	58.96	81.42	107.92
2	5.31	11.44	18.49	26.58	35.82	46.35	71.92	104.70	146.43
3	5.41	11.96	19.85	29.30	40.57	53.97	88.66	136.96	203.75
4	5.52	12.52	21.33	32.36	46.11	63.19	110.41	182.07	290.10
5	5.63	13.11	22.95	35.83	52.60	74.35	138.78	245.57	421.56
6	5.74	13.73	24.71	39.74	60.19	87.91	175.94	335.51	623.42
7	5.86	14.38	26.63	44.16	69.08	104.41	224.76	463.54	935.50
8	5.98	15.06	28.73	49.15	79.51	124.50	289.08	646.53	1420.58

*ROR = Rate of Return

AN EXAMPLE TO TEST YOURSELF USING IIA-1: You want to accumulate $50,000 in 20 years and want to know how much you would need to invest each year if you plan to increase your investments 1% each year and your investments earned 5% a year. (ANSWER: $50,000 / 35.83 = $1,395)

IIA–3: This table assumes the annual investment amount will increase 3% per year (AIIPY = 3).

TABLE IIA-3

3% AIIPY	YEARS ANNUAL INVESTMENT WILL BE MADE								
ROR*	5	10	15	20	25	30	40	50	60
0%	5.31	11.46	18.60	26.87	36.46	47.58	75.40	112.80	163.05
1	5.41	11.96	19.85	29.30	40.57	53.97	88.66	136.96	203.75
2	5.52	12.49	21.21	32.02	45.32	61.59	105.40	169.23	261.06
3	5.63	13.05	22.69	35.07	50.82	70.70	126.68	212.81	343.20
4	5.74	13.63	24.30	38.50	57.21	81.61	153.90	272.28	462.80
5	5.85	14.25	26.05	42.36	64.63	94.73	188.90	354.17	639.38
6	5.97	14.90	27.95	46.70	73.27	110.54	234.12	467.88	903.20
7	6.08	15.58	30.03	51.59	83.34	129.62	292.81	626.83	1301.37
8	6.20	16.30	32.28	57.10	95.09	152.71	369.25	850.35	1907.31

*ROR = Rate of Return

AN EXAMPLE TO TEST YOURSELF USING IIA-3: You want to accumulate $50,000 in 20 years and want to know how much you would need to invest each year if you plan to increase your investments 3% each year and your investments earned 5% a year. (ANSWER: $50,000 / 42.36 = $1, 180)

IIA–5: This table assumes the annual investment amount will increase 5% per year (AIIPY = 5).

TABLE IIA-5									
5% AIIPY	YEARS ANNUAL INVESTMENT WILL BE MADE								
ROR*	5	10	15	20	25	30	40	50	60
0%	5.53	12.58	21.58	33.07	47.73	66.44	120.80	209.35	353.58
1	5.63	13.11	22.95	35.83	52.60	74.35	138.78	245.57	421.56
2	5.74	13.66	24.44	38.91	58.19	83.69	161.07	292.53	513.27
3	5.85	14.25	26.05	42.36	64.63	94.73	188.90	354.17	639.38
4	5.96	14.87	27.80	46.22	72.05	107.85	223.90	436.07	815.96
5	6.07	15.51	29.70	50.54	80.63	123.48	268.19	546.07	1067.38
6	6.19	16.20	31.76	55.38	90.55	142.16	324.57	695.28	1430.85
7	6.31	16.91	34.00	60.82	102.05	164.52	396.72	899.48	1963.36
8	6.44	17.67	36.44	66.92	115.40	191.36	489.48	1181.14	2752.60

*ROR = Rate of Return

AN EXAMPLE TO TEST YOURSELF USING IIA-5: You want to accumulate $50,000 in 20 years and want to know how much you would need to invest each year if you plan to increase your investments 5% each year and your investments earned 5% a year. (ANSWER: $50,000 / 50.54 = $989)

Appendix G:

DREAM LIFE SPENDING PLAN

– IN CURRENT DOLLARS

LIVING EXPENSES	*Monthly*	*Quarterly*	*Annually*	
Rent / Mortgage				
Home Maintenance/Repair				
Utilities				
Phone				
Furnishings/Household				
Regular Clothing				
Special Clothing				
Laundry/Cleaning				
Groceries				
Eating Out				
Auto Payments				
Auto Insurance				
Gasoline/Transportation				
Auto Maintenance/Repair				
Entertainment/Club Dues				
Subscriptions/Cable, etc.				
Vacations				
Leisure Activities				
Health Insurance				
Medical/Dental Costs				
Legal/Financial Costs				
Life Insurance				
Other Insurance				
Gifts				

School Costs/Daycare				
Donations				
Other				
Other				
SUBTOTAL				
Multiply By	12	4	1	
SUBTOTAL				
Plus 10% MISC.				
TOTAL EXPENSES				
ADD COLUMN TOTALS TO GET AN ANNUAL TOTAL				$

Made in United States
North Haven, CT
10 November 2026

22088264R00152